D0116486

978.0075 Mac

COWBOY AND GUNFIGHTER COLLECTIBLES

By Bill Mackin
Photos by Nancy S. Bostain

MOUNTAIN PRESS PUBLISHING COMPANY
MISSOULA, MONTANA

Library of Congress Cataloging-in-Publication Data

Mackin, Bill.
    Cowboy and gunfighter collectibles : a photographic encyclopedia with price guide and maker's index /
Bill Mackin ; photos by Nancy S. Bostain.
      p.   cm.
    Includes index.
    1. Frontier and pioneer life—West (U.S.)—Collectibles—Catalogs. 2. Cowboys—West (U.S.)—Collectibles—
Catalogs. 3. Firearms—West (U.S.)—Collectors and collecting—Catalogs 4. Cattle trade—West (U.S.)—
Equipment and supplies—Collectors and collecting—Catalogs. I. Bostain, Nancy S. II. Title.
F596.M17 1989   89-3416
978—dc20   CIP

Mountain Press Publishing Company
P.O. Box 2399
Missoula, MT 59806
1-800-234-5308

DEDICATION

To the many old-timers—like Roy Olson at Boise, Red Bunn at Rifle, Chuck Roberts at Craig, Henry Schaefermeyer at Vernal, Pax Baker, the old sheriff at Leadville, and Mrs. Goldie LeFevre right here in Meeker — who told me their stories and sold me their spurs.

TABLE OF CONTENTS

Preface

My original price guide in *Cowboy and Gunfighter Collectibles* underpriced most items. Among the various comments I received about it, both good and bad, one stands out: A noted Texas collector simply offered me double the price-guide figures for my whole collection. I respect a man who puts his money where his mouth is, but I kept the collection.

There is more to establishing a value on a collection, however, than simply determining its price. Among my more treasured items is the braided kangaroo bridle with glass buffalo head rosettes. I once made a decision in Rock Springs, Wyoming, whether to buy it for thirty dollars or to have enough money to put gas in my old truck to get back to Salt Lake. I still have the bridle.

The only Winchester '73 rifle I've kept was sold to me by the late Charles Guild of Evanston for fifty dollars. Charlie's grandfather had once used the gun to hold Wild Bunch miscreant, Bob Meeks, for the Uinta County sheriff, but Charlie couldn't understand my wanting it. "Thirty-two twenties," he advised me, "won't even kill hogs very well."

My favorite spurs were sold to me by Roy Olson, a real gentleman in the cowboy meaning, who sold me a lot of his life-long accumulation over several successive annual Boise gun shows. Sure, inside they're marked Morales, but the greatest kick in publishing my book was sending Roy his copy.

More recently Tom Hyde, a prominent Santa Gertrudis breeder and crack marksman from Ohio, retired to New Mexico and sold me his gun belt. He tells me it's the last one actually made and tooled by his old friend, Tio Sam Myres. I didn't know S.D. Myres, but I have the pleasure of knowing Tom Hyde.

An item's *value* might not be reflected in its price.

Certainly the price guide had to be updated, and I didn't have to think twice about the best man for the job. The Museum of Northwest Colorado chose Brian Lebel to appraise my collection when they accepted it to establish The Cowboy and Gunfighter Museum in their building. Brian is the most knowledgeable cowboy artifacts dealer I know. He understands values, not just prices.

I've watched Brian grow in and with the business for several years, and I have great respect for his knowledge, his acumen, and his ethics. While he indeed has the heart of a collector, he also has the head of a shrewd dealer. He rarely misses a show or an auction, and he deals nationally, not just in the West.

While he was appraising my collection at the museum, Brian put what I thought to be an exorbitant figure on my worn but fancy Hamley chaps. Now, I like those chaps. I first spotted them on an old cowboy when I was a kid mustanging near Stockton, Utah, and was pleased to get them some twenty five years later from the cowboy's son. But Brian's figure was about triple my own estimate.

When I told him I thought the figure was too high, he said, "Want to sell them to me?" That's Brian Lebel, another guy ready to put his money where his mouth is.

About the New Price Guide

Cowboy gear is uniquely American. Perhaps this explains our great interest in collecting it.

Collectors are drawn toward western Americana for a variety of reasons. Some grew up watching Western movies; others love history; still others appreciate western art. The "Wild West" didn't last long, and the articles people used during that brief period are hard to come by, mainly because most of the things were used hard to perform necessary work. The realm of cowboy collectibles has expanded beyond the earliest opening of the West; it now extends well into the twentieth century and, of course, centers on the massive cattle industry.

As you review the new price guide in *Cowboy and Gunfighter Collectibles*, remember that while this remarkable collection belongs to just one man, it represents an overview of the whole field. In addition to the fine pieces that constitute this collection, there are many more items and even more variations of each to consider.

The prices listed here are based only on the photographs you see in the book. Slight variations in the condition or style may result in drastically variable pricing. Also, previous ownership of an item by some particular person may affect its price. To simplify the matter in this book, each item is priced without regard to previous ownership.

These prices reflect my knowledge of the current market for like items, using reasonable auction and show prices. Prices change as more collectors come into the market and the supply fluctuates.

Brian Lebel
Cody, Wyoming

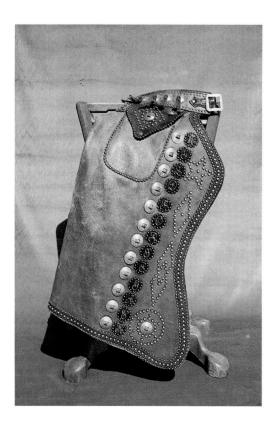

"I see by your outfit that you are a cowboy. . ." This exceptional collection includes chaps by R.T. Frazier, Pueblo; Colorado prison spurs, Canon City; Heiser cantina or pommel bag holster; and saddle by Frank Bregenzer.

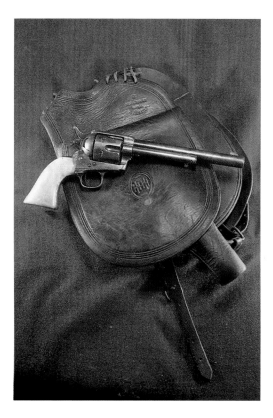
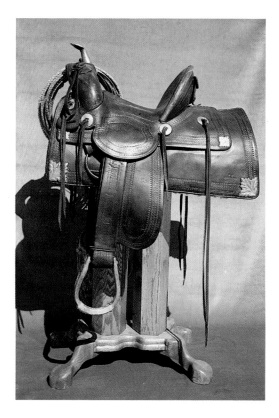

BY WAY OF INTRODUCTION

First off, let me own up; I'm not really a cowboy. Like many of the Saturday matinee generation, my first introduction to cowboys was the movie version presented in our urban Dallas theater. By the fourth grade, my fresh-from-Texas manners and obvious horse craziness had made me a frequent and not too unwelcome nuisance at the old J.W. Jenkins saddle shop in downtown Salt Lake City. There, in that aroma of leather and musty horse sweat, I met and listened to the old men who had lived the legend.

Blessed then with years full of horses, dogs, guns, and the room to use them, my fascination grew. I read voraciously. While I appreciated the romantic legend, I was even more impressed with the real history and lore. I became a devotee of Will James, but a student of Jo Mora. I tried cowboying, of course, but frankly wasn't much of a hand. I even tried a little contesting on rodeo rough stock but was thoroughly convinced by age twenty that it's a whole lot more fun to play cowboy than to be one. I had already lbecome what I really am, a collector.

Like many collectors, I'm critical, but no legend has survived as much debunking as the cowboy's and the gunfighter's. I feel no need to add there. Like all collectors, I'm a romantic, but again, no subject has been so thoroughly romanticized as this. Let me share instead what I have learned from and about his tools, gear, and possession— those items that have become the cowboy collectibles.

I've presented the gear in an alphabetical arrangement, thinking it the most convenient, and I've tried to include a little history and collector information with each section. As for values, I claim no great scientific research, just a feel based on nearly forty years of swapping and accumulating. Many, no doubt, will think my prices much too conservative. Well, I've been to some of those auctions too! Others, I'm sure, will find them too high. Pocket-book permitting, I always like to add a nice item. If I'm too high, talk me down; I'm usually willing to pay less.

Sincerest thanks to those who have helped with this effort, especially my friend, boss, and photographer, Nancy S. Bostain, my friend and secretary, Kathy North, and my best friend and wife, Mickee.

Bill Mackin
Meeker, Colorado

ADVERTISING

The American cowboy has been called the hardest working icon in advertising. After all, he has sold everything from Cream of Wheat to sports cars, peddling B.B. guns to kids, beer to dads, and music to moms for decades. He has sold tobacco for more than a century—Marlboros alone for thirty-five years now—and whiskey since the 1870s.

Of course, he is used mostly to sell to other cowboys or would-be cowboys, as in the famous *Last drop from his Stetson* ad (see Catalogs, photo #96). Nearly from the beginning, the cowboy has been a rather style conscious fop led by dime novelists and Wild West showmen, by painters, by movie makers, and by rodeo producers. The cowboy has been the main consumer as well as the author of his own legend.

Collectors will find a wealth of material in the advertising area. Movie bills and movie star related materials are a huge specialty. The old Wild West shows used lots of promotional material and their old lithographed advertising is a fascinating, but expensive pursuit. Cowboys or Old West characters in beer ads alone would fill a collection, and the early cowboy cigarette cards nearly predominate cards of baseball players.

(SEE WATCH FOBS, CATALOGS)

1) *Tex and Patches* is one of the cowboy in advertising classics. Actually a sheriff (note the six-pointed star behind his kerchief), Tex and his ewe-necked horse were painted by Frank E. Schoonover and owned and distributed by the Colt's Patent Fire Arms Company in the 1920s and 30s.

2) A pot-metal rendition of Buffalo Bill rides in front of a small Miller Bros.Real Wild West poster. Actually not a cowboy himself, the hard-drinking Bill Cody and other flamboyant promoters brought the cowboy mystique to international fame. The statue sold at Wild West shows for a dollar.

3) Jo Mora's famous cowboy poster of 1933 is the author's personal favorite. Distributed by Visalia Stock Saddle Company until the 1940s, a later re-issue sold blue jeans. Along with his book, *Trail Dust and Saddle Leather,* Jo Mora's posters and art have inspired many to become collectors.

BADGES

Law badges are very popular among Western collectors, and, while not strictly cowboy items, their history parallels the armed horseman from medieval times. Badges became prominent in the days of heraldy and knighthood when they were worn both on the knight's armor and on his horse.

The Latin roots of *constable* mean "master of the horse," a mounted law man. *Marshal* comes from the Teutonic word for horse, and sheriffs were originally knights appointed by the English king to uphold peace.

In the American West, badges varied greatly. Some were literally homemade tin stars, and some were exquisitely crafted jewelry. Most were commercially manufactured, and many, called *stock badges,* were standard catalog or drummer-sold items that might be used anywhere.

Badges are difficult to date precisely, but the pin offers a clue. If original, a one piece bar with pin and catch denotes a badge made after 1937. It will usually have patent numbers. A safety pin soldered to the badge is usually early, especially if not covered with a plate, but most early badges will have separate pins and simple catch findings.

In general terms, badge values depend on age, design, material, and the rank and location of the police officer. A sheriff's badge would generally be more valuable than his deputy, and notorious Old West locations excel. Western collectors seem to prefer stars to shields, and the simpler styles tend to look older even if they're not. Hallmarks or maker marks also add value. A name on the badge may help date and authenticate it. Ownership by a particularly famous, or infamous, lawman adds value, of course, but documentation must be thorough. Notarized statements are themselves often fakes.

In this area of collecting, fakes and reproductions outnumber the genuine articles. Beware of badges made from copper and those representing the more famous Western towns. Indian police badges are popular fakes. Recent reproductions are often fine quality castings of old authentic badges. Few old badges are completely cast. Look for enameled lettering and authentic wear.

4) Western deputy badges include *Sutter County* (California), stamped nickel with enameled lettering, safety pin with plate closure, hallmarked *Patrick Moise Klinkner Co., San Francisco*.

Bexar County Texas, sheet brass with separate stamped plate, enameled letters, patent pin.

Salt Lake County, Utah, stamped nickel with separate copper seal in center, patent pin.

Moffat Co., Colorado, cast bronze material with enameled state seal in center, soldered separate pin and clasp, *Hi-Glo*.

5) Railroad police badge from Chicago, Burlington and Quincy Railroad, Nickel-plated brass, safety pin with plate, hallmarked *S.D. Childs & Co., Chicago*.

City Marshal stock badge, Cast German silver, separate center, altered pin, has one ball broken.

Rio Blanco Co., (Colorado) *Sheriffs Posse*. Stamped nickel, patent catch, hallmarked *Sachs-Lawlor Denver*.

Salt Lake County Sheriffs Posse. Stamped nickel, patent catch, hallmarked *Salt Lake Stamp Co*.

Horse-mounted sheriff's posses remained prevalent in many Western counties until recent years but are being replaced by jeep rescue groups.

6) *Chief of Police, Bingham Canyon, Utah.* Nickel shield with gold star and lily in center, two piece catch, hallmarked *Salt Lake Stamp Co.* Name *M.L. Ewing* engraved on back. Bingham Canyon was a notorious mining town in the 1870s. It was finally closed by the growth of Kennecott Copper's open- pit mine.

Bingham Canyon, Police Chief. Nickel with gold- plated star and wreaths, screw back for use on hat. Hat badges are less popular.

Utah State Prison. Nickeled shield with brass state seal, altered pin, hallmarked *Salt Lake Stamp Co.*

Corrections Officer, Wyoming State Prison. Nickeled with separate state seal, two-piece pin and catch.

7) *Salt Lake City, Special Police, 1464.* Stamped sheet steel, safety pin with cover.

Special Police, 476, Salt Lake City. Nickel shield with separate star center, two-piece pin, hallmarked *Salt Lake Stamp Co.*

The value of both these badges is reduced by the word *Special.*

Express 144. Hand-lettered nickel shield, heavy safety pin with cover, reportedly used by an express company in Denver.

City Marshal stock badge. Plated brass with stamped design, safety pin without cover.

8) *Constable, Bunkerville Twp., Claren Leavitt.* Cast brass with enameled Nevada state seal, late two piece pin and catch.

Utah Indian War Veterans Medal 1856-1872.

Town Marshal, Ophir, Utah. A good quality cast reproduction sometimes sold as genuine, patent pin.

Deputy U.S. Marshal. Nickeled brass, safety pin with cover, authenticity doubtful.

BELTS

"The cowboy never wore galluses, and he rarely wore a belt to support his trousers," wrote Emerson Hough in 1897, "but he did wear a belt, this the wide, heavy leather belt that carried his pistol holster." Indeed, the cartridge belt is a sometimes overlooked item that has received recent and emphatic interest among collectors of cowboy memorabilia.

American in origin, the cartridge belt dates from the Revolutionary War, but saw its greatest era of use and development in the post-Civil War years in the West, when self-contained metallic cartridges emerged. The 1870s and 1880s saw the introduction of numerous textile cartridge loop designs to overcome the problem of leather-caused verdigis on copper cartridge cases. These were used extensively by cavalrymen and hunters.

Of greatest interest to most collectors of cowboy memorabilia, however, was the development of the combination cartridge and money belt. The bodies of these belts were usually folded over and stitched closed, making a long pocket, and many early Westerners, always suspicious of paper money, carried their savings in gold or silver at their waists.

A later type of belt associated with the cowboy is the riding or *bronc buster*, or sometimes *kidney* belt, which seems to have been a popular item with rodeo rough stock riders from the 'teens through the 1930s. These are wide bands of leather, usually with two or three buckles, which were said to give extra support to the lower back. These, too, are becoming collectibles.

Bright sashes, as worn by artist Charles Russell, were popular with Westerners dating back to the fur era. Some beautifully woven ones originate with the Indians of Mexico, and highly decorative belts called Squaw Belts were made of extensively beaded buckskin among the Utes and Shoshones.

Finally, the more modern cowboy belts, for instance the Ranger sets with horseshoe-style buckle, retainers, and tab, as well as big trophy buckles, are becoming increasingly collectible, especially those crafted by the fine old silversmiths.

(SEE GUN RIGS)

9) A variety of cartridge belts that orginated in the 1870s and 1880s include from the top:

Model 1876 U.S. Prairie belt. A combination of canvas and leather, marked *Watervliet Arsenal, A.R. Smith.*

Model 1880 U.S. Mills belt. A patented all-textile belt with a cast, quickly-detachable buckle. Quick-release buckles saved lives fording rivers.

Civilian Mills woven belt with "dog-head" buckle in wider, rifle-caliber size. Narrower, revolver-cartridge size. Both military- and civilian-style Mills buckle plates are extensively faked.

Scarce Winchester "bear-head" cartridge belts in wider, rifle- and narrower, revolver-cartridge sizes. These are marked *Patented Feb. 15, 1881. Manufactured by the Winchester Repeating Arms Co. New Haven, Conn. U.S.A.*

10) A variety of early cartridge or gun belts include, from the top:

Mail-order quality .38 caliber belt. It has a leather strip sewn as a block for cartridges and early-style embossing at edges.

A .32-20 caliber belt with separate tongue and buckle billets.

Brigham Patent marked .38 caliber belt. Tapered-tongue, laced-through rather than stitched cartridge loops, and some basket-weave embossing.

George Lawrence Company—Portland Oregon USA marked. .45 caliber, laced-loop, tapered-tongue belt.

Money and .32-20 cartridge combination belt. The body is folded pigskin, stitched at the top and at the tongue end. When the tongue goes through the slot behind the buckle, the money pocket is sealed.

Large, wide belt for both long rifle and revolver cartridges.

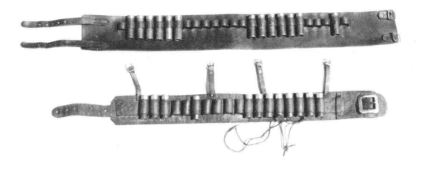

11) Two more all-leather cartridge belts. These are for 12-gauge shotgun shells. The bottom belt is tooled and has rigging for shoulder straps and the popular California or garrison buckle style.

12) Various riding or *bronc buster* belts, which came into vogue in the 'teens after cartridge belts had largely disappeared.

Top: A ranch-made belt embellished with the Texas star. Several of the nickel-plated brass studs have worn through from many years use in Utah's Unitah Basin. Center: Commercial, russet-leather bronc belt with edge embossing. Bottom: Another commercially-made belt with floral-embossed edge pattern, marked inside *Keyston Bros. San Francisco.*

13) A fancy, embellished bronc-riders' belt from the 'teens or 1920s. It has edge binding, embossing, and numerous nickeled studs. The swastika and triangles are hand-worked alloy, possibly indicating prison manufacture. The swastika, once prevalent in decoration of cowboy gear, disappeared with the rise of the Third Reich in the 1930s. Some items, such as spurs, were multilated to remove it.

14) Two fancy nickel-spotted bronc belts. The top one is felt-lined and made by Gallup and Sons, Denver. The lower one is by Lawrence at Portland, Oregon.

15) Ute beaded squaw belt on white buckskin. Whether worn by Indian or white, these ultimate waist-sashes are strictly for show.

BITS

The use of bits by horsemen dates to prehistoric eras, and the collecting and study of bits is extremely widespread. Those bits most identified with the cowboy follow the general division of cowboys west and east of the Rockies.

In California, the *vaquero* first hackamore-broke his mount, then introduced the showy, heavy Spanish spade bit, or, later perhaps, the half-breed, a somewhat gentler modification with a roller or *cricket* mounted in the mouth port. He might also use a ring bit or *chileno*, with which an iron ring fits in the mouth port and circles under the horse's chin, effecting the same purpose as a curb strap. In any case, his bit would have rein chains, a holdover from the days of knighthood when leather reins were easily cut. It would likely be embellished with inlaid silver, and it would reflect its Spanish ancestry.

The plains cowboy broke his horse with the bit and used a gentler instrument on his animal. The influence of military bits on the post-Civil War plains is apparent, and many cowboys used the popular U.S. model 1859 or the later Shoemaker bits. One regional development was the Texas curb bit, a short, curved shank bit with solid rings and mild port, which permits the horse to graze while bridled. The plains steel bit has solid or moveable rings for the direct attachment of the leather reins.

The ornate California spade bit is unquestionably the most desireable to cowboy tack collectors. Early specimens are usually of blued, hand-worked iron, often of a loose-jaw or flexible design, and usually represent beautiful inlaid, engraved silver work. They are rarely maker-marked, but marked ones may bring a premium.

Later bits will show more commercial short cuts and machine work and are more frequently maker-marked. The support bars that run up to the spade usually have coiled copper wire rather than individual copper pieces. The silver work and quality may continue to be very high or rather ordinary, and values vary accordingly. Some very nice early-style blued bits are being made in Mexico and imported.

Though perhaps more military items than cowboy, those cavalry bits with brass U.S. medallions on their shanks are popular and valuable with cowboy memorabilia collectors. They have been reproduced for at least 60 years. To ensure value, look for military inspection or arsenal marks, and beware of replaced brasses.

Among the Texas bits, the most popular are those by famous makers. McChesney, Kelly Bros., Shipley, and Crockett predominate in the era between the World Wars, and Renalde and Ricardo became prominent in the 1940s. Those bits with figural shanks like gal-legs and those made of bronze or adorned with silver, brass, gold, etc., command highest prices. Overlay rather than inlay predominates plains-style mounted bits except for some desireable items made in Western prisons.

With some competition, but without true peer, the August Buermann Mfg. Co. of Newark, New Jersey, dominated bit and spur manufacture for decades, beginning with their founding in 1842. Their famous star brand is found on bits of virtually all styles—California, Texas, and others—and in virtually any quality, as their catalog states, *from the cheapest to the very best*. Buermann was acquired by North and Judd (Anchor Brand) about 1920, but manufacture of many Buermann styles and use of the Star Brand continued into the 1960s. Early Anchor bits of nice quality may also be found.

A reprint of Buermann's catalogue No. 35 is available, as is Crockett's #12 and an early Kelly Bros. Substantial information about several notable "Texas" bit and spur makers is available in the out-of-print *Old West Antiques and Collectibles*. Information on the most notable of marked California bit shops, G.S. Garcia of Elko, Nevada, is available in the book of that name. Garcia, a saddle maker, employed such notable California bit and spur makers as Juan Estrada, Asabio Herrera, Philo Gutierrez, and Mike Morales.

(SEE BRIDLES, SPURS)

16) An early Santa Barbara California, spade bit. It has 4¼"-high spade mouth with a copper roller. The support bars are covered with individual pieces of copper. It is extensively engraved, silver-inlaid, and mounted with domed silver buttons. It was a lifelong treasure of the late Frank Longtine, Wyoming cowboy and spur maker.

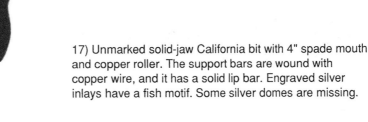

17) Unmarked solid-jaw California bit with 4" spade mouth and copper roller. The support bars are wound with copper wire, and it has a solid lip bar. Engraved silver inlays have a fish motif. Some silver domes are missing.

18) Loose jaw, Santa Barbara-style California bit with 3½" spade mouth and roller. Support bars are wound with copper wire. Engraved silver inlays and domed buttons. Though unmarked, this is an early mass production copy, probably by August Buermann.

13

19) Commercial, Santa Barbara, solid-jaw spade bit with 4"
spade, roller, copper-wire-wound support bars and nickel spots
on chased cheeks. The roller was thought to amuse the horse
and copper to give the animal a sweeter taste than iron.

20) *H. Messing. San Jose, Cal.* marked bird-head-style half-
breed bit with missing roller, solid lip bar, and the rein chains
typical of California bits. This early bit has exceptional graved
cheeks and quality.

21) Spade bit by August Buermann called the *Arizona* in
early saddle catalogs. This one was ordered along with
#23 from Hamley in 1916.

22) Unmarked, but probably Buermann bird-head-style half-breed bit with roller. The half-breed is a modification of the more severe spade bits. The holes above the mouth bar in this commercial bit permitted its manufacturer to use either mouth. They would receive the support bars in a spade bit.

23) Buermann's #406 silver-inlaid, half-breed bit cost $7.00 in 1916, or fifty cents less with chain rather than malleable bar.

24) This Santa Barbara-style Buermann bit was No. 397, the *Star*. It was available with either spade or half-breed mouth.

25) August Buermann No. 1373 Buffalo Head California bit with half-breed mouth. This star-brand bit is made from what Buermann called *Hercules Bronze* with nickel silver ornamentation. The buffalo head is the most popular with collectors of a series which also include a horse head, spots, a star, and an Indian chief.

26) Mike Morales' No. 36 Las Cruces-style bit sold for $18 in 1925. Morales was first in Pendleton, then Portland, Oregon, after leaving G.S. Garcia about 1910. Most of his bits are marked with his famous squashed M on the Mouth bar.

27) This beautiful silver-inlaid concho and crescent bit has had the mouth altered to a simple port bit.

28) An unmarked Las Cruces-style port mouth bit with solid lip bar and engraved silver inlays and conchos. This California bit was used with rein chains. Loops for a curb strap have been added. Alterations decrease collector interest and values.

29) U.S. Civil War Model 1859 Cavalry bit marked, *Allegheny Arsenal, 1864*. The bit has brass U.S. medallions, a curb chain, and a medium-high port mouth.

30) U.S. Indian War Model 1874 Shoemaker bit marked *RIA*. This bit has smaller brass U.S. medallions and a very low port.

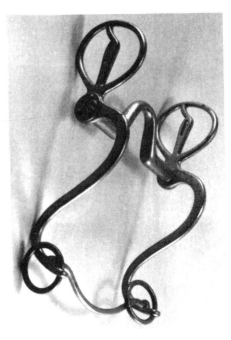

31) Despite its U.S. medallions, this old Buermann bit is not a military Shoemaker. Copies of U.S. bits have been made for many decades. Check for inspector's initials.

32) U.S. Cavalry Model 1909 curb stamped *1, B.T.C., U.S.* It has a curb chain and low port mouth. The number 1 refers to mouth size and numbers run 1 through 4.

33) Buermann star-brand bronze curb bit. Basically a Texas curb bit with bar mouth. *The diamond head and beveled-edge cheeks* were patented in 1914 and called Panama bits.

34) *Crockett* marked mild port-mouth Texas curb bit. It has engraved silver alloy hearts and bars mountings. Most silver-mounted bits from the Plains states are overlaid rather than inlaid and use alloy rather than silver.

35) Highly collectible *gal-leg* style curb bits. To the left, a *Kelly Bros.* marked bit with engraved silver and gold overlays. To the right, an unmarked silver, copper, and gold-mounted bit by the probable originator of the gal-leg style, John Robert McChesney.

36) Small Texas port-mouth curb bit with engraved silver heart mountings. Unmarked bits or spurs of uncertain source are usually called *shop-made* by collectors.

37) Contemporary *Hall* silver and copper-mounted gal-leg port-mouth curb bit. Interest in old bits and spurs has led many contemporary makers to imitate the old styles.

38) Old cast-metal, gal-leg bits. These were obviously a popular item of Victorian *porn* and could be mail-ordered from Montgomery Ward or Sears in the 1890s.

39) Shop-made high-port curb bit. This nude female figure has been carved from aluminum bars, as was the heart-motif lip bar. Aluminum bits have limited interest to collectors.

40) The popular *rearing horse* bit. Unmarked, but probably by North and Judd (Anchor Brand), this bit is nickel-plated iron with solid lip bar.

41) Early Mexican *chileno* or ring bit. The ring fit around the animal's lower jaw.

42) Silver-inlaid, Mexican curb bit with port mouth and rein chains. It originated in the mountains of Jalisco.

43) Very intricate, small, Mexican curb bit. Its half-breed-type mouth is jointed and has copper strips. The end pieces are silver coins, and it retains remnants of silver inlay.

44) Contemporary, Mexican, gal-leg bit with half-breed mouth, curb and rein chains, and coins mounted at the ends of the mouth bar. Mexican bits, like California ones, show the Spanish heritage of rein chains.

45) Unusual commercial mule ring-bit of nickeled iron. Mule bits have narrower mouths than those intended for horses.

46) Unmarked, but probably North and Judd (Anchor Brand) chased and cadmium-plated roping bit. The low lip bar is designed to prevent the rope from coming up to injure the horse.

47) Late *Crockett* sterling-silver-mounted grazing bit. Like most American makers, the once huge Crockett firm is no longer in business.

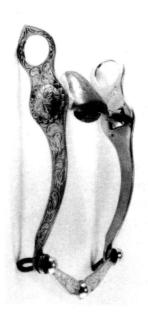

48) *Garcia* full-engraved, silver-overlaid bit with humane roller mouth and lip bar. Most collectors prefer the old blued bits to more modern stainless ones.

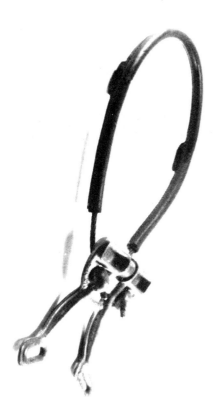

49) One of several patented hackamore bits which have no mouth bar, the *San Angelo Easy Stop* is made of cast aluminum alloy, steel cable, and leather.

BLANKETS

Colorful Navajo blankets and rugs, though obviously Indian items; appeal to almost all Western collectors. Already a two-hundred-year-old craft with these cousins of the fierce Apaches, weaving began to decline in the early reservation era. It was revived largely through the commercial efforts of several post traders through design changes, broader marketing, and the inception of using Navajo weavings as rugs rather than just for wearing blankets.

By the early 'teens, most large saddle shops were selling Navajo woven-wool saddle blankets by the pound. Hamley's catalog #10 offered single- or double-size saddle blankets for $1.40 per pound and floor rugs at $1.75 to $2.25 per pound. The prices were still almost identical in 1940. Since weaving a double saddle blanket, which might average around six pounds, took a Navajo woman some 140 hours, exclusive of the time to clean and card the wool, these blankets were true bargains. Sales of these *pound blankets*, however, contributed to another decline in quality because care and design were so little reinforced.

Serious Navajo blanket collectors recognize about a dozen reservation areas with characteristic colors and styles, and they seek diligently the rare pre-reservation-era blankets. Less serious ones seem to like the color and style, and even the lowly old *pound* saddle blankets are of interest for their Western flavor.

Blankets of similar styles have been imported from Mexico for years. Though these vary greatly in quality, none seem to engender as much interest as the Navajo items. Current saddle blanket copies from Mexico sell for as little as $20.

Older blankets or rugs often have seen use, and condition does, of course, affect the value. Damage can be repaired at the owner's discretion, but please, never, never wash a Navajo rug!

50) A fairly nice *pound blanket*-era double saddle blanket colored in tans and dark brown. Fairly loose in weave, it would have sold for about seven dollars.

51) This more colorful example of a double saddle blanket has red, black, and greys. Dimensions of double saddle blankets vary from about 28" to 34" wide with lengths approximately double the width.

52) Like most reservation-era blankets, this double saddle blanket has a border and an alternative use as a throw rug. The early weavings had no borders and were all wearing blankets.

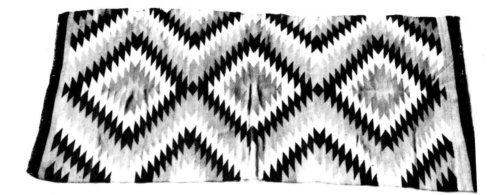

53) This larger 3' x 5' weaving is a combination of browns. Though definitely a rug size, this well-woven item shows use as a saddle blanket.

54) This larger 4' x 5' rug has a very intricate tapestry pattern and is a combination of browns. Such items have been collectibles since early this century, and Navajo women continue to produce a few.

BOOKS

The variety of books in demand with collectors of Old West and cowboy items is vast. Books about, by, or used by cowboys all have their followings. Early dime novels, which helped generate the legend, are valuable, and the somewhat less glamorized biographies that followed are invaluable to more serious researchers.

Older books by artists Remington and Russell are highly collectible, and the first edition illustrated novels of the latter-day *Lone Cowboy*, Will James, have a loyal cult of followers. Other early fiction, especially books illustrated by the more prominent Western artists, have collectible values, as do those that created Hollywood legends like Hopalong Cassidy.

Cowboys were likely to have a working familiarity with at least two books besides the saddle catalogs. These were the brand books published in all Western states and the tally book. Brand books were a record of all registered brands and ear marks within the state, together with the registered owner's name and location. Originally a county record in most areas, registry became state-wide by the 1890s in Wyoming and in 1924 in Nevada.

A tally book was usually a pocket-sized notebook in which the cowboy or rancher kept business notes, herd counts, brand information, or even his diary.Some have various logs for gauging the weight of cattle and aging horses and include listings of railroad tariffs, bank rates, and other information helpful for the cattleman. A well-used tally book is a real find for the collector of cowboy items.

(SEE CATALOGS)

55) Some books with varying historical significance include:

My Life on the Range, 1924, by Scottish-born Wyoming ranch manager John Clay.

Thirty-one Years on the Plains and in the Mountains, 1900, by Western scout and Indian fighter Capt. Wm. F. Drannan.

Ten Years a Cowboy, 1898, by C.C. Post, which has an attractive cover and illustrations.

Buffalo Bill and His Wild West Companions, a romanticized biography autographed by Buffalo Bill and Eugene Field.

56) Inside fly of *Buffalo Bill* shows an autograph of Cody and the book plate and signature of Eugene Field, author and book collector, dated Sept. 14, 1895. Though Cody was not a cowboy, Buffalo Bill items are highly collectible among Western collectors.

57) A paperback Nevada Brand Book of 1946 and hardbound Colorado 1948 edition. These were working tools for ranchers, brand inspectors, and shippers, and they are becoming popular collectors' items.

58) Wyoming Brand Books from 1912 through 1956 with supplements. Substantial Western history and heraldy are recorded here.

59 & 60) This tally book, given away by the Denver Union Stock Yards Company, has a 1916 calendar and numerous logs of use to cattlemen. It has notations of brands entered and a list of what are probably railroad car numbers. It was used by a working cowboy at Rifle, Colorado.

BOOTS

The attributed parentage of the cowboy boot is almost as diverse as its lore. In both Texas and California, the very earliest cowboys likely wore wrapped buskskin leggings above moccasins or even sandals. Later, *botas-de-ala* were worn. These were that early form of puttee often seen in Frederick Remington sketches. This *bota-de-ala*, or winged boot, was often fringed, embroidered, or decorated like the half-breed legging of the mountain man and Indian, and it was at least a precursor of the fancy Hollywood cowboy boot.

It should be noted that the Spanish Conquistador to the south had brought a thigh-high boot from Europe, complete with high heel and long pointed toe. A very similiar boot was revived by Buffalo Bill and other Wild West showmen in the 1880s. Impractical for real cowboys, it was widely known as the stage-driver boot.

Further east, high-heeled boots with European cavalier ancestry were common with Southern planters. The flatter-heeled Wellington style was a standard among even urban gentry, and some variation of it was a cavalry standard around the world. Most drovers through the 70s wore these flat-heeled boots.

Among the craftsmen drawn to the cattle trails were boot makers, including Hyer of Kansas and Justin in Texas. Legend attributes the development of the true cowboy boots to them. An early style called the *Coffeyville* (Kansas) boot was made of soft kid leather, had a top band of a contrasting color with an embroidered star or horseshoe, high heels and tops, and was closely fitted to either right or left foot. Most earlier boots would fit either foot.

The cowboy boot of the 1880s was marked by a high, square-cut vamp, high, straight-cut *stove pipe* top, and high heel. The soft leather top was usually of calfskin and came up to just below the knee, 15 or 16 inches above the heel line. The top was stitched in parallel rows or, later, in patterns to stiffen it.

By the 1890s the heel of cowboy boots tended to be more under-sloped and its front sat farther forward under the side seam. In this same era, the scalloped top with varying depth of vee front and back emerged, along with a lower, scallop-shaped seam between the vamp and boot top. The toe became generally more pointed.

At the turn of the century, a somewhat lower top with inlaid white leather became popular. Cowboys of this era were more likely to wear pants outside their boots or to hang their trouser leg in the scalloped vees. In the 'teens and 1920s, Hollywood and rodeo influenced the styles to the extreme. Colors were sometimes outlandish and the inlay leather-work extensive. One popular style of the 1930s was the low-topped Pee-Wee boot.

The cowboy's high heel, goes the legend, helped hold the stirrup without sliding through and helped him dig into the earth when holding roped animals on foot. The pointed toe finds the stirrup easily. High heels do give a little ground clearance for spur rowels. Importantly, they add a little stature to a group of men who, though truly tall in the saddle, tended to be pretty short afoot.

The survival rate of old cowboy boots is poor, and collectors are eager to find pre-1900 examples, even in worn condition. Later boots by prominent or artistic makers are also in demand. Collectible pre-war boots are always of natural leathers and have heels of stacked leather pieces. Lower walking heels are thought to be late and not collectible.

61) These early true cowboy boots have 2" heels set well behind the side seam, rounded toes, and calfskin tops that have a stitching pattern to stiffen them. These boots were used by a member of the Forman family of Heber, Utah, and probably date about 1880. The vamp, or boot front, comes to the straight seamline well up the 14" top. The spurs, also early, are unmarked hand-forged, with silver and copper inlays and fancy graved-silver overlaid buttons. They have one-piece, dove-wing straps.

62) These boots, circa 1890, have more under-sloped 2" heels, set farther under the side seam-line and 13" pattern-stitched stovepipe tops. The vamp, still fairly high, is stitched to the top in a scallop pattern. Their pointed toes have been capped. They belonged to a cowboy in the area of Grand Junction, Colorado, and are only about size 4. The spurs are Indianola style with leather-covered bands. The straps are studded with nickeled brass spots.

63) Around the turn-of-the-century, leather inlays around the top and a vee-cut top pattern emerged. The vamp and top seamline became generally lower and deeply scalloped to run even with the heel counter and top seam. Dating boots with these features becomes more difficult. This pair has 1 3/4" under sloped heels and 10" tops. The spurs are plain Ricardo nickel-silver steel with 1 1/2" nine-point rowels. Ricardo's soldered construction is sometimes called a *three piece* spur.

64) This very fine quality pair of movie-era boots was made in Tucson, Arizona, about 1925. A wingtip style adorns the toe and a butterfly the extensively stiched top. The spurs are Buermann's Star Brand double gal-leg in Hercules Bronze.

65) In the late 1920s, a deep-vee-cut, low-top boot called the Pee-Wee became popular. Like many later innovations, it was more suitable in the arena than on the range, where the low top funneled in flipped-up rocks and dirt for the working cowboy. This pair was made by Kirkendall of Omah, Nebraska, one of several fine and now collectible makers, circa 1930.

The spurs are shop-made, straight-shanked working spurs with attractive wide basket-weave and concho straps. Nice straps add value to spurs.

66) The Hollywood influence prevails in this pair of Mexican-made boots of bright yellow, red, and two-tone green. They have very undersloped 2 1/4" heels, 9" tops, and exotic crocodile toes. Circa 1935. Though unmarked, the spurs are attributed to Al Matson, Redding, California. They are full-engraved-silver overlaid, and have 1 1/4" saw-tooth rowels and a contoured-heel fit.

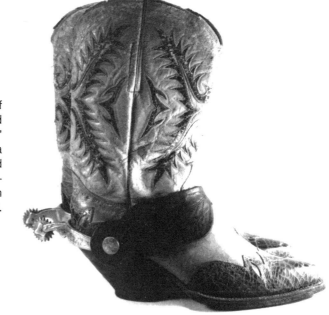

67) Laced boots find little interest with collectors, but old photos show many cowboys wearing them. In this case, a cowgirl, Goldie LeFevre, of Meeker, Colorado, wore these on the family ranch in Axial Basin about 1915. Shop-made by Meeker blacksmith, George LeFevre, these long-shank, Rocky Mountain-style spurs are graved on one side and have 1 1/2" five-point rowels. George gave these to Goldie as an engagement present in 1916.

BRANDING IRONS

The branding of cattle in North America traditionally began with the three crosses brand of the conqueror, Hernando Cortez, more than four and a half centuries ago. In fact, virtually all European emigrants to the New World were familiar with hot-iron branding to mark ownership of animals, but in the vast unfenced West, branding became the stuff of legends.

Early cattle brands in the West were often drawn with a running iron. Usually large, these free-hand efforts were best adapted to most early simple brands. Later, more complex brands necessitated the use of the stamp iron. Indeed, attractive brands which are well worked out not to blotch easily are registered, assessed, taxed, and sometimes sold for high prices in the West.

Often maligned and sometimes even outlawed, the running iron holds a fascination for most collectors. Running irons have various shapes and styles, including some very inventive ones, but all are predicated on moving a curved surface over the hair of the animal.

Stamp irons vary from simple bar or curve, parts of a design, to very intricate patterns. In either case, the iron is designed to be pressed against the animal's skin rather than moved across it. Most are made of iron, but some may have a heat area of copper or even aluminum. The majority have fairly long handles with a ring end to facilitate hanging them up. American branding irons sometimes have a wooden handle over the metal to protect from heat. Branding irons with a wooden handle that slips into a metal socket usually originated in Mexico.

Stamp irons also vary greatly in size. Large figures are usually for cattle, smaller ones for horses. Even smaller brands were sometimes used on horse's jaws or even hooves. Some care must be exercised to distinguish these from various other marking tools, such as log stamps.

Collectors are most interested in hand-wrought branding irons, those made before welding became widely available. Their intricate design and workmanship make some of these true examples of folk art. Branding irons documented to represent famous or notorious ranches are also desirable, as are those used by the U.S. Government. Fakery becomes an issue in these categories.

(SEE BOOKS)

68) From left: Hand-forged iron with a wooden handle over the iron rod. This iron stamps an ox yoke pattern 2 1/2" x 6", is only about 17" in overall length, and is said to have originated in Virginia about 1830.

Next, a hand-wrought running iron with curved nose and straight working edges, 21" overall. Numerous styles of running irons were made.

Right: A commerical stamp iron marked *D.M. Franklin Serum Co.* The 4" U stamp is made of brass. The 12" steel handle unscrews to make a very compact unit for horseback use.

69, 70, 71) A variety of hand-wrought, stamp branding irons. Handles average over three feet long and have a circle or crook at the top for hanging up the iron. Branding irons with socket-style handles, twisted shafts, and complicated unintelligible patterns are likely from Mexico.

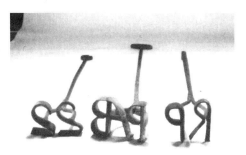

BRIDLES

Bridles are among those items that reflect the marked difference in cowboys west and east of the Rockies. The vaquero of California and his buckaroo kin in Oregon, Nevada, and Utah hung their heavy spade bits in almost flimsy, narrow-cheeked head stalls, often sewn round and adorned with silver. Their reins, likely braided rawhide, were of one piece, attached to bit chains at the front and a romal or quirt-like extension at the back. Reins were left on the horse's neck when he was tied by the *mecate*.

The Texan cowboy and his followers on the plains conversely hung their small bits in heavy, wide, leather-head stalls. Their reins were long, flat, separate leathers that attached directly to the lower rings of their curb bits. The horse was sometimes tied by his reins, or they were simply dropped, and the well-broke horse was considered *ground tied*.

The intricate, braided horsehair bridles usually made in Western states' prisons are very popular with collectors. Braided leather or rawhide bridles are also collectible and may show varying amounts of intricate craftsmanship. Other bridles are valuable because of extensive silver work or other adornments. The more common "using" bridles seem to get little attention unless stamped by particularly famous makers.

(SEE BITS, REINS)

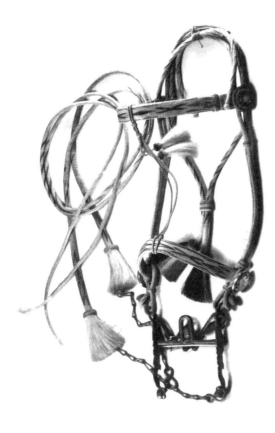

72) A tri-color, mane horsehair bridle made at Wyoming State Prison, Rawlins. The bridle has round work cheeks, throat latch with tassels, split tapered reins, flatwork brow and nose bands, and two pairs of glass bridle rosettes. Condition is very fine. Horsehair braiding called *hitching* may be the most intricate and beautiful of all Old West folk art.

73) Another Wyoming prison bridle from Rawlins, this piece has extensive flat hitch work in a leather headstall. The reins, too, are a combination of plaited leather and horsehair.

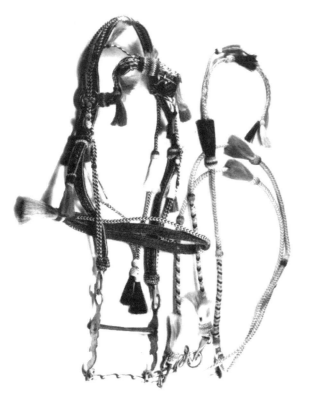

74) A very colorful horsehair and synthetic fiber bridle believed to have been made at Colorado State Prison, Canon City. It is primarily flatwork and has round California-style reins and romal. Like many horsehair bridles, it uses little hardware in its design. Condition is excellent.

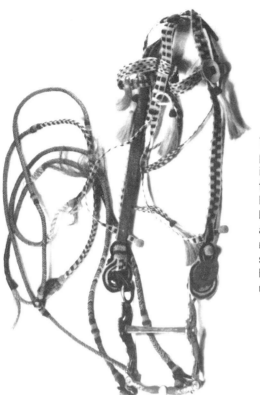

75) Another Canon City prison bridle, this one is black-and-white flatwork stitched onto leather cheeks. The buckles are handmade and graved, and the round reins are separate. This bridle has seen substantial use and some damage.

76) This combined leather and horsehair headstall is also from the Rawlins prison. It has four glass rosettes in leather braid and numerous tassels.

77) Once a very fine piece, this tri-color, round-work bridle has faded with use. The romal is now missing from its round, California reins. It has no hardware other than the bit and glass horsehead rosettes. It is thought to have originated at Washington State Prison at Walla Walla.

78) An intricate and finely-braided headstall of very thin, finished, leather strips. The bridle is completely adjustable with sliding leather pieces and braided Turks heads. It has no hardware other than the buffalo-head rosettes and bit.

79) A simple, very colorful California, round-work horsehair headstall with large tassels. Light-colored mane hair has been dyed yellow and red in this piece. The reins and romal are not original to it. It is believed to have been made at Idaho State Prison, Boise.

80) This is a simple, heavy-leather, plains-style bridle and humane bit made collectible by the *Kansas City Stock Yards Co.* legend stamped across its brow band.

81) An extreme example of the plains style, this very heavy, double, edge-laced leather headstall has extensive engraved silver adornments, including card suits, swastikas, and a horse head. The buckles are handmade silver laminated to brass.

82) A typical light California headstall with engraved silver buckle and adornments. Split ear-bridles in which one or both ears held the crown piece in place were common to both California and Texas schools.

83) Basically similar to California bridles, this contemporary Mexican leather headstall has been stitched with red and black wool. Its reins would likely be twisted horsehair, one piece, and likewise adorned with colorful wool.

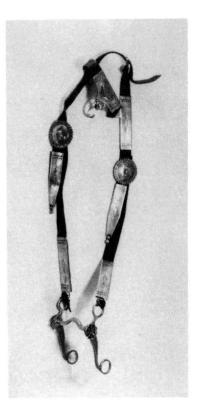

84) Truly a piece of *horse jewelry*, this Navajo Indian-made bridle has extensive tooled and turquois-mounted silver over leather cheeks and brow band and a *naja*, the horseman's famous crescent. Even the bit appears to be sand-cast silver.

CARTRIDGES

Old ammunition has received substantial collector interest in recent years, and individual specimens, boxes, and advertising items, especially the old cartridge display boards, all have a following. Cowboy collectors are usually most interested in boxes of ammo that might have been used in popular cowboy guns, the Colts and Winchesters.

Earlier ammunition boxes are of a two-piece or pull-apart design. Some very early ones will have a wooden block inside the cardboard box. Labels can sometimes be dated by the lithographer's code date. Values will depend on the maker, desireability of the caliber, and condition and completeness of the box and its contents. Most early boxes illustrate the cartridge, and those that picture a firearm seem especially desireable.

(SEE BELTS, COLTS, STINGY GUNS, WINCHESTERS)

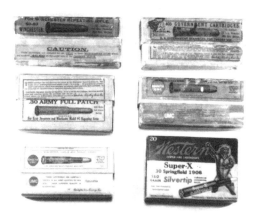

85) A group of full cartridge boxes for large, lever-action Winchester rifle models 1876, 1886, 1894, and 1895. The earliest box, upper left, has a wooden block reinforcing the cardboard box. The latest, lower right, has side opening flaps, and the cartridges slide out in their divided cardboard tray.

86) Various styles of boxes for the smaller thirty-two-twenty (.32 W.C.F.) from the 1880s to 1940s. Model 1873 and 1892 calibers were usually packed fifty to the box. With the exception of the 25.20, these calibers were also chambered in Colt revolvers.

87) A group of full cartridge boxes for Winchester's 1894 Model. Though most famous in thirty-thirty (.30 W.C.F.), this workhorse was chambered in five calibers by 1904.

CATALOGS

Saddle catalogs, the cowboy's bibles, are largely a post-1900 development. Though a few saddlers may have published catalogs as early as the 1880s, most then used photo cards to show their line. Sporting-goods dealers were generally earlier to get in on the boom in mail order merchandising, and their catalogs often include a lot of cowboy items, as do those of the general merchandise houses like Sears, Roebuck and Co. and Montgomery Wards. By the 'teens, however, virtually all of the large, successful saddle houses were issuing catalogs, and it can be surmised that this was a major source of sales until the 1940s.

Earliest catalogs tend to be rather sparse and matter-of-fact in content, but by 1915 Hamley Saddles, for example, was including E.A. Brinstool cowboy poetry within its 164 pages of saddles and gear. *Hamiley's Cowboy Catalog* in 1925 had pictures of rodeo cowboys within and without and a few books on cowboy lore. By the 1935 edition, clothes and a company history moved saddles to the middle of the catalog, and Will James, the author who claimed to have learned to read from saddle catalogs, joined the book page.

That same year of 1935, Visalia Stock Saddle Co. offered tips on anthrax from a veterinarian, the famous Jo Mora poster map of cowboy lore, and page after page of exquisite silver-inlaid spurs and bits. It is obvious why these old cowboy wish-books have become wish-books for today's collectors. In a general way, they reflect the regional and time differences that make up the lore of cowboy collectibles.

Old catalogs of guns, boots, sporting goods, and other cowboy-used gear are also desirable. Condition and size, as well as artistic covers, add to the appeal, and therefore value, of old items. Primarily, however, they are research tools, and the very early and rare items with greatest historical significance to the West are the most valuable. Some catalogs of bit and spur makers and many gun catalogs have been reproduced.

(SEE BOOKS)

88) Photographic studio cards, such as this one from the J.A. Donnel shop in Rawlins, Wyoming, pre-dated catalogs for most saddle makers. Information on the back makes it clear Mr. Donnel encouraged mail-order business.

89) Early catalogs by notable makers are desirable and rare. These date from about 1910 to 1927.

90) These catalogs are full of Indian items in unbelievable quantity and date from the early 1900s. Full-beaded moccasins are offered at $12 per dozen pairs.

91) Three early catalogs in excellent condition include R.J. Andrew, 1914, featuring saddles and Kelly Bros. spurs. Hamley's 1925-1926 catalog with Wallace Smith's famous bronc picture on the cover, and a 1920s Visalia catalog with extensively silver-mounted California gear.

92) From the 1930s catalog from Vasalia, Hamley, N. Porter, and the Read Brothers. Most share similar items like Crockett spurs but also reflect substantial regional differences.

93) A series of catalogs from the same maker are valuable in dating cowboys' gear and price fluctuations. These Hamley catalogs date from about 1915 to 1941.

94) This group of catalogs all came from the famous N. Porter Co. in the 1930s. Some unmarked items can only be identified by old catalog pictures.

95) Three smaller, stapled catalogs from Denver in the 1930s. The Heiser catalog in the center is entirely of holsters and gun leather.

96) In the 1920s and 1930s, several merchandisers put out cowboy catalogs. Increasingly, the emphasis was on general gear and clothing. Values are incremented by exceptional art, like the famous J.B. Stetson Hat Co. painting on this Stockman Farmer.

97) Another group of 1930s general stockmen's catalogs. The older Mueller Saddle and Harness became Saddles and Ranch-wear.

98) Late-1930s catalogs reflected the changing nature of the business. While capitalizing on the traditional bronc-riders for covers, the catalogs often emphasized heavily silver-mounted parade horse equipment inside.

99) Another group of catalogs from the late 1930s and 1940s. Many of these note the lack of materials, special taxes, and other difficulties of war-time production.

100) By the 1950s, many of the old makers were gone, and catalogs were used more in scattered retail outlets than by mail-order purchasers. A very few, like J.M. Capriola, Elko, Nevada, continue to produce saddle catalogs for working cowboys.

101) A group of catalogs from the famous H.H. Heiser Company. Heiser began publishing separate gun-leather catalogs in the early 'teens and dated their founding from a very debatable 1858.

102) Another famous maker of gun leather and fine saddles, S.D. (Tio Sam) Myres, also published separate catalogs. These date from the 1940s.

103) An early sporting-goods catalog with at least some interest to Westerners, this Thomson & Son, New York, effort offered mail-order items in 1878.

104) One of the West's most famous sporting-goods jobbers, Browning Bros. of Ogden, Utah, did a large mail-order business with cowboys and other out-doorsmen. Their first catalog date is unknown, but 1905, left, is catalog #40.

105) Mail-order sporting-goods catalogs of East or West were also popular bunkhouse reading. These four all date from the 'teens.

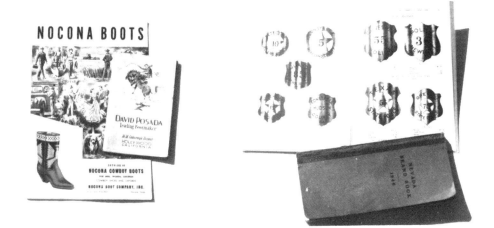

(106, 107) Manufacturers of boots, hats, badges, guns, and other miscellaneous cowboy collectibles also sometimes issued catalogs. Each contributed to the area of Western lore and collecting.

108) Bit and spur maker catalogs have taken on a special interest to collectors of cowboy items. North and Judd were major makers, and Mike Morales was famous for his quality. The original No. 3 price list complements the recently reprinted No. 5 catalog.

109) A group of reproduced catalogs by prominent bit and spur makers. All have been reprinted in the 1980s.

CHAPS

The cowboy's chaps, like so much of his gear, represent the blending of some traditional antecedents. The Mexican vaquero developed some large leather shields, or *armas*, which hung from the front of his saddle and protected both horse and rider from the thorny chaparral. The Mexican, Indian, and Anglo Westerners all found advantages to buckskin or other leather trousers or leggings. The earliest cowboy chaps were simply seatless trousers or leggings made of leather heavy enough to turn the thorny brush, *armas* worn by rider rather than horse.

These early chaps are usually topped by a straight belt, laced in front and buckled in the rear. They often have pockets stitched on their fronts and sport fringe down the outside seam of the legs. Later ones will often have conchos running down the seam as well. Called "leggins" by their Texas originators, collectors have developed the name *shot guns*, referring to the double-barreled appearance of their closed legs.

A variation of shotgun chaps called *woolies* became popular in California and the Northwest. In these, the hides of angora goats, bears, or other animals were lined and used for the leg front. These *hair pants* added to the water-shedding ability and warmth of the closed-leg chaps, and, not infrequently, to their aroma as well. They were popular throughout the North Country by the 1890s.

A final style of chaps, the Texas-wing or bat-wing style, became popular by the turn of the century. Rather than a closed leg, this style was held by several fasteners or snaps permitting easier removal and better ventilation. Evolution of this style has been toward fewer closures, lighter leathers, and fancy rodeo styling.

Collectors' interest in old chaps lies mostly in the early shotgun styles and woolies, but interest in fancier old batwings seems to be increasing. As with most leather collectibles, maker cartouches on the belts are very important to value.

Chap belt-fronts show a general progression from a straight line, laced juncture to a dipped, single-grommet style designed to break away easily. Post-war chaps frequently have a light belt arrangement in front. While age is not the only factor, collectors tend to like the earlier styles.

110) Very typical early closed-leg or *shot gun* chaps by Victor Marden, The Dalles, Oregon. Note the straight belt-line and "spaghetti" fringe down each leg.

111) Anglos, Indians, and Mexicans all found use for leather britches. These buckskin pants were worn by a Mexican vaquero. Since they could be easily pierced by thorny chaparral, he would likely wear *armas* or *chaparejos* over them.

112) This hard-worn, old pair of H.H. Heiser chaps were used by Maybell, Colorado, cowboy C.A. Roberts about 1920. The right pocket has a hole in the back that permitted the 71/2" barrel of Mr. Roberts *coyote medicine* to run down along his leg.

113) These superb shotgun chaps came from the shop of S.C. Gallup, Pueblo, Colorado. They are extensively tooled, fringed, and buckstitched, and have been preserved in very nearly new condition.

114) F.A. Meanea, Cheyenne, Wyoming, made this beautiful pair of long-haired, black angora chaps in 1895 and shipped them to Elmer Jackson of Lehi, Utah. They are still in nearly new condition.

115) These new condition H.H. Heiser gold angora chaps are youth size and inscribed in ink inside the belt "To Brother from Daddy, April 9, 1916." They have the single-hole, break-away front.

116) This red-brown pair of Miles City Saddlery chaps were acquired by Ray Bates of Gila, Arizona, in 1947. Despite their late date, they have the early, four-hole lacing style. Ray gave his hair pants substantial use.

117) These white angora chaps were made by O.J. Snyder, Denver, Colorado. They also have a laced, but dipping, belt front. Angoras came in a variety of natural and dyed colors.

118) These fancy, batwing-style angora chaps were made by Lawrence at Portland, Oregon. Spotted angoras were made by sewing in pieces of contrasting colored hide and are sometimes called *pintos*.

119) These very unusual woolies are actually made from the shoulder hair of a buffalo. The late belt-style indicates that they were probably made from an old robe, and the hide has some dry rot. Old chaps made from bear, horse, and other hides are not uncommon.

120) Roy Olson, a buckaroo now retired in Boise, special-ordered these extra-wide batwings from Al Furstnow at Miles City, Montana about 1930. They have the breakaway front and, like all of Roy's gear, show use but care.

121) These fancy Hamley, Pendleton, Oregon chaps with rearing horse conchos and lots of nickel spots were cataloged around 1925. The wear is compliments of Utah's western desert country.

COATS

Though not frequently evident in the Hollywood movies, the Old West did have winters, and cowboys did wear coats. Even the vests seen most frequently in old photos are fairly substantial garments; indeed, they were short, sleeveless waistcoats. Blanket-lined jackets and ponchos were not unknown in some areas, and the famous *Fish Brand* pommel slicker, basically a sailor's rain gear redesigned to cover man and saddle, saw use throughout the West.

For winter blizzards though, a true overcoat was needed, and it was often made of hair on animal hides. Early on, this might have been of buffalo like those used by U.S. troops in Montana, but by the late 1880s, most were of horsehide.

Like many items of clothing, collectors will find the old cowboy vests and coats were expendable and now scarce. The old slickers especially deteriorated easily, and one in presentable condition is a rarity. The heavy fur overcoats, however, have more frequently survived in good condition and make interesting additions to an Old West collection.

122) An exceptionally nice quality overcoat, this black horsehide model featured braid and bar closures, a closely quilted lining, and a large roll collar. It was made by Gordon & Ferguson, St. Paul.

123) This old coat originated in Douglas, Wyoming. Though shaggy like a bear-skin, it is more probably from a winter-killed horse. Though other hides were sometimes used, and raccoon became very popular by the 1920s, most early coats were buffalo or horsehide.

124) A broadside advertisement and price list for the Chicago Hide, Fur, and Wool House of Douglas, Wyoming, the makers of the coat in photograph #123, is shown with the smaller 25-page catalog of Globe Tanning Co., Des Moines, Iowa.

125) This simpler, plainer, and, no doubt, less expensive horsehide coat has no label. It has loop and button closures and an unquilted lining. None of the pictured coats have the split-tail design of pommel slickers and the recently revived dusters.

COLTS

Of all cowboy collectibles, simply nothing transcends the Colt revolver. From the improbable history of the illustrious inventor, Colonel Samuel Colt, who was only very technically a colonel and not really the revolver's inventor, through the very real commendations of the early Plains Indian fighters, to the fantasy and gorgeously engraved hardware of latter-day Hollywood heroes, Colts fire up collectors!

Colt's first revolvers, those produced in the 1830s by Patent Arms Manufacturing Co. of Paterson, New Jersey, included both handguns and rifles, established the revolvers' reputation as the plainsman's weapon, and became collectors' items long before the cowboy era. The Walker model, Colt's 1847 effort at Whitneyville Armory, was his first and biggest six-shooter and was born of the Mexican War and Texas Ranger urgencies. Both of these early models tend to carry price tags that look like phone numbers.

A variety of percussion arms followed through the Civil War years and experimentation with cartridge guns came afterwards. Colt's progress here was severely restricted by patents held by the competitor firm, Smith and Wesson, until 1869. After that date, a raft of small pistols and *conversions* — cartridge hand guns usually not really converted but simply employing parts of the earlier percussion models—were manufactured.

By 1877, the Colt firm was manufacturing a double action and added the modern side-swing cylinder in 1889. Colt's ultimate pistol, the John Browning patented semi-automatic, began in 1900. Concurrently, Colt manufactured several cartridge long arms, including two shotgun models and a rare double rifle. Of special interest to most Old West collectors are the three slide-action, repeating rifles and the scarce Colt-Burgess lever action rifle and carbine.

But the pistol that has become virtually synonymous with the Wild West cowboy and gunfighter is the Colt Single Action Army and Frontier Revolver, or, more simply, the Model P. Manufactured originally from 1872 until 1940, demand for the traditional old *Peacemaker* created many imitators, and finally spurred new production of the Old Colt in the 1950s. At least six books have been written covering the pre-war single actions, and a couple have appeared covering the post-war guns. Variations, calibers, and collector lore all seem endless.

Of course, just as with the Winchester rifle, cowboys did carry other side-arms. Most of Colt's competitors through the 1870s, 1880s, and 1890s made big, single-action, frontier revolvers. Besides Smith and Wesson, these included Remington, Merwin and Hulbert, and Hopkins and Allen. They all, however, seemed to receive substantially less favor from cowboys then and collectors now.

Colt collecting is very definitely its own specialty, and most Colt collectors are very fussy about originality, condition, and rarity. It is imperative that Colt collectors learn to distinguish original finishes and patina. Because Colts get "pricey" the fakers get skilled. There is, fortunately, a lot in print about Colts and an old collectors' adage of "buy a book for every gun."

On the other hand, the demand for old cowboy stuff has seemingly created interest in lower-condition guns, ones with cut barrels, even the refinished items. Many of Colt's competitors, including the Belgian and Spanish copies, look great on the wall or in an old holster and certainly cost less.

(SEE GUN RIGS, STINGY GUNS, WINCHESTERS)

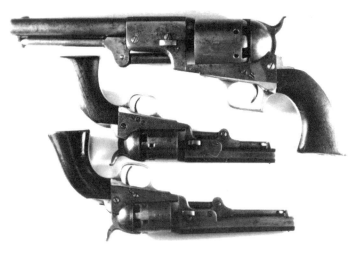

126) Successors to the famous Walker, Colt's big Dragoon revolvers were among the first products of his Hartford plant. This early specimen incorporates Whitneyville parts and is known as a "Fluck Dragoon." Below are two variations of the 1849 Pocket pistol. One is a five-shooter, rather than six.

127) Probably the most appealing of all percussion Colts, the Model 1851 .36 Caliber Navy revolver is also one of the most common. Colt values are hurt by damage, such as on the grip of the middle revolver, and modifications like the non-factory sight on the bottom one.

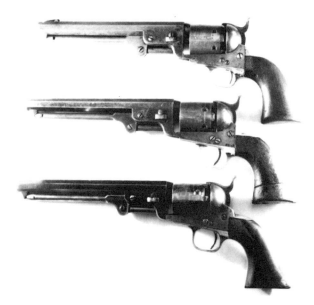

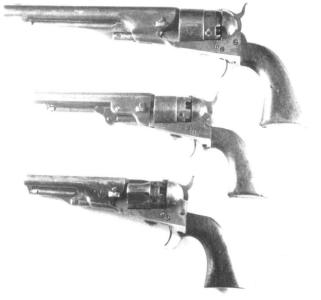

128) Workhorse of the Civil War and very common in the holsters of Westering cowboys and gunmen, the top revolver is the .44 caliber 1860 Army. Below are the Pocket Navy and Police models of 1862.

129) This Richards-style 1860 Army in .44 center fire and a 31/2" round barrel Pocket Navy in .38 rim fire are representative of a substantial group of Colts usually called "conversions."

130) Basic old Colt .45's are this very early U.S. Cavalry model (center) in a range reputedly issued to Custer's troops; the U.S. Artillery model, Cavalry models later refurbished, cut to 51/2" barrels, and reissued to the troops; and a fine condition civilian *Peacemaker* made in 1881 (top).

131) These two worn, old single-actions are both veterans of the cattle trails, and both were used in pre-1900 killings. The nickled gun is in the scarcer .38 Colt caliber.

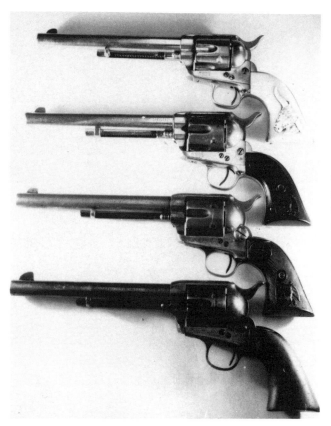

132) The *Frontier* model usually refers to those single-actions in 44.40 caliber. These four range from 1881 to 1913 vintage. *COLT FRONTIER SIXSHOOTER* was first etched, later roll-stamped on the left side of this model's barrels. The caliber was developed for Winchester's famous Model 1873 rifle and used in both arms by many cowboys.

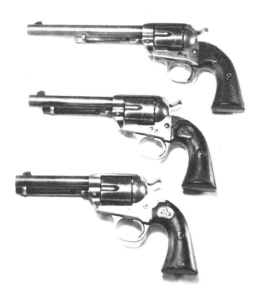

133) A close cousin of the single-action Army and numbered in the same serial number range, the Bisley Model also came in standard barrel lengths of 43/4", 51/2", and 71/2". Originally a target model, the later standard-frame Bisley was popular with turn-of-the-century Westerners.

134) Though produced in some thirty different calibers, the single action's most common were .45 Long Colt, 44.40 (or 44 W.C.F.), 38.40 (or .38 W.C.F.), 32-20 (or .32 W.C.F.), and the .41 Colt. These basic 43/4" barreled, smokeless powder guns all date about 1900 and represent the cowboy's big five.

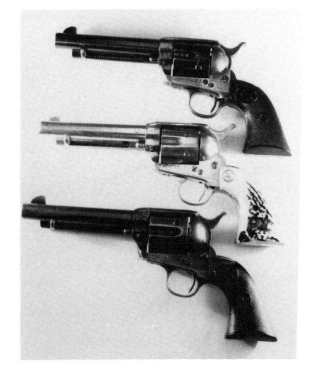

135) These three Colts are medium length, 51/2"-barreled, smokeless-powder guns. There is a sliding transverse pin holding the cylinder pin, as opposed to the screw from the front of the frame on the earlier black-powder guns. The bottom gun is a scarce variation that has longer cylinder fluting.

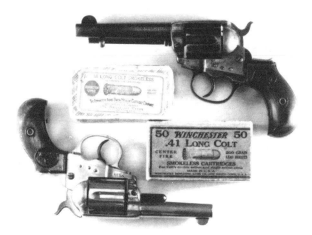

136) Colt's first double-action revolver, the Model 1877 *Lightning*, was most often chambered for .38 and .41 Colt cartridges. A much smaller gun than the single-action Army, it has been traditionally linked to Billy the Kid, who reportedly favored its diminutive size.

137) Colt's next introduction was the big Model 1878 Frontier double-action revolver, chambered for calibers similar to the single-action Army from 32-20 to .45 Colt. A variation of this big revolver was the Model 1902 U.S. Ordnance *Alaskan* or *Phillipine* revolver shown at the bottom.

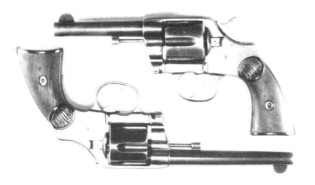

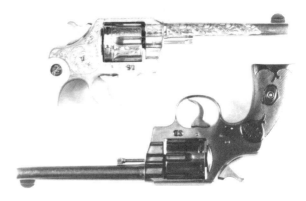

138) Though a hundred years old, these Model 1889 *side swing* double-action revolvers look quite modern. While later double-action models have not found much favor with collectors, a lot of them saw use in the old timers' holsters.

139) Army Special Colts were descendants of the 1889 Navy and antecedants of Colt's Official Police. The top gun is factory engraved, has carved pearl grips, is .41 Colt caliber, and was shipped in 1916. The plain blue gun is in 32-20 caliber.

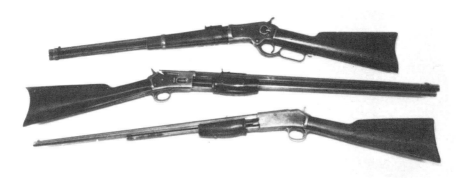

140) Colt made rifles, too! Among numerous models of long guns manufactured by Colt are this rare Colt-Burgess "Baby" Carbine; a medium-frame, slide-action Lightning rifle, .38-40 caliber; and the small-frame Lightning slide-action .22 caliber rifle.

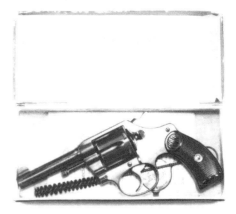

141) Colt's biggest cartridge hand gun, the New Service, dwarfs two New Police Double Action revolvers in blue and nickel. These are all turn of the century continuations of the side-swing-cylinder models.

142) Original boxes and paperwork add value to early Colts like this old Pocket Positive .32 New Police.

CUFFS

Those writers of Western lore who maintain absolute practicality in every item of cowboy garb seem especially strained to account for his leather cuffs. Contrary to some opinion, leather cuffs cause shirt sleeves to wear faster, and rope burns occur on the palm, not the wrist. The truth is that cowboys wore cuffs for the most obvious of reasons: to look like cowboys.

Cuffs were an 1880s outgrowth of the large gauntlet gloves favored by early cowboys and style-wise horsemen back to the medieval knights. They remained intermittently and regionally popular through the 1920s and early 1930s. New ones are again being manufactured.

Collectors are especially eager to acquire cuffs by famous makers. Fakery is a problem, but unlike most other leather collectibles, post-1900 cuffs may have a snap that bears the maker's name, as well as a stamped cartouche in the leather. Fancy embossing, studs, spots, and conchos also add appeal.

(SEE GAUNTLETS)

143) *R.T. Frazier, Pueblo, Colo.* is stamped on the outside top edge of these 8" cuffs, as well as on the Frazier snaps. They are in new condition with their original price penciled in *$1.10.*

144) These 7" cuffs have a *Heiser-Denver- HHH* snap. Different styles of Heiser closure snaps are seen, and all are post-1900.

145) *Frank Bregenzer, Maker, Rifle, Colo.* marked 61/2" cuffs have a hand-stamped, ribbon-edge design. Bregenzer was once an employee of W.R. Thompson Co.

146) This pair of lace-and-snap-style 7" cuffs was made by Snyder Saddles Denver. Their edge embossing is floral leaf design.

147) This 7" pair of cuffs has rivets and snaps marked, *Gopher Brand—DFB Co.* The longhorn steer motif is machine embossed.

148) Hand-tooled with an Indian head, this 7" pair of cuffs shows substantial use. The bottom edge has been serrated to give them a little stretch.

149) Nickel spots or studs became very popular by the 'teens and 1920s. Older ones are plated brass, not steel. These 8" cuffs have scalloped tops and some basket-weave tooling.

150) 7" cuffs with buckle closures, nickeled spots, and nice floral tooling that were owned by the late Bob Glen of Boise, Idaho.

151) These hand-tooled, ribbon-design 61/2" cuffs each have three snap closures with swastikas. Once popular on cowboy gear, swastikas disappeared in the 1930s. They may indicate manufacture by Newton Porter of Phoenix.

152) These smaller 6" cuffs with beautifully tooled Indian-head and floral design show years of wear. They have buckle closures.

153) Made for a woman or youngster, these 5" cuffs have a geometric-pattern edge design. Youth or lady-sized gear usually has less collector appeal and value.

154) This exceptional pair of 7" cuffs was made and marked by T. Flynn of Pueblo, Colorado. They feature nickel spots in the Texas star pattern and conchos with strings.

GAUNTLETS

The gauntlet or wide-cuffed glove of the Plains cowboy was definitely rooted in cavalier traditions. "Originally," noted Jo Mora, "the cowboy was a gloved knight, and in his daily routine of riding, roping, branding, etc., the flying fringes of his gauntlets gave an accent to his costume that was mighty picturesque and distinctive." Even the embroidered, fancy cuff-back was a tradition predating the cowboy by hundreds of years.

Virtually all plains horsemen wore gauntlets until cuffs and the shorter *roping* gloves supplanted them. Early catalogs offered them, usually emblazoned with the Texas star, horseshoes, or steer heads. By the 1880s, reservation Indians were selling them widely. These were made of fine, smoked, tanned buckskin and usually had extensively beaded patterns. They have remained available on Western reservations to the present.

Collectors seek both the commercial and Indian varieties, but the extensively beaded, white buckskin gloves prevail in value. The short-cuffed roping gloves also have some collector interest. These, too, were sometimes made on reservations. Finally, the long-cuffed gloves or mittens made of beaver, muskrat, or hair-on cow or horsehide were a working cowboy item on northern ranges and are now collectible.

(SEE CUFFS)

155) An early and excellent pair of cowboy gauntlets, reportedly made for Buffalo Bill. They are probably Shoshone in origin.

156) Large smoke-tanned elkskin gauntlets. Their unusual floral style is typical of Gosiute work in Nevada.

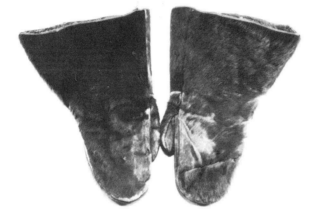

157) An old pair of worn cowhide farriers' mittens. Such items saw much cowboy use in northern latitudes.

158) Both of these pairs of gauntlets are thought to have originated in the Plains states. Cowboys often bought beaded items on reservations, and early mail-order catalogs made them available everywhere.

159) An unusual lady's-size pair of commercial cavalry gloves, Apache beaded with initials and 1st Cavalry insignia.

Small and plain Ute beaded gauntlets.

GUN RIGS

Though holsters in the broadest sense are virtually as old as pistols, those used by the cowboys and Western gunfighters are associated with the development of the revolver. The heavy Colt Walker and Dragoon revolvers were most often carried on the saddle's pommel. In fact, the engraved cylinder scenes of these big "Holster Pistols" illustrate that style of use. Colt soon manufactured a model called a pocket pistol and, in 1851, the Navy Belt Pistol. A similar name and size distinction had also existed with his earlier Paterson models.

Earliest U.S. military belt holsters seem to have originated with the 1851 Navy, and civilian styles for this model are much more common than for the big Dragoons. All military and most civilian percussion-era holsters featured full flaps, which amply protected the gun. An exception was the early Slim Jim or California holster.

This early, open-top holster often incorporated beautiful vine-and-leaf-style carving. The toe often had the sewn-in plug closure. The back of the pouch had a belt loop, sometimes sewn but usually secured with two-piece copper rivets. Unlike their military contemporaries, these holsters were usually right-hand-draw and russet rather than black in color. They were very infrequently maker-marked, but Western makers do predominate.

These closely contour-fitting holsters remained popular in the early years of the big cartridge, frontier revolvers as well. The lines were adjusted to the ejector rod housing and head, and the open, S-curved top cut deeply at the trigger was retained.

At about this time another style of open-topped holster, the Mexican loop, evolved. In this holster, cut entirely from one piece of leather, the pouch was pushed through slots in the back flap, eliminating the need for a belt loop. In its various configurations, the Mexican loop holster was to become the cowboy standard and the most popular of collectible holsters.

With the proliferation of cartridge arms came several variations of cartridge belts, both leather and textile. One popular style, the folded and stitched calf or pigskin belt that was designed to carry money inside, has become very popular with collectors.

Meanwhile, the Old West gunmen experimented with the old notion of shoulder holsters and a new fast-draw idea of hanging the pistol on a belt-mounted clip. These, and the later ideas of pocket holsters, release devices, and clam shells, had greater interest to lawmen and other professionals than to the working cowboy.

An enormous escalation of interest and price has been evidenced in the last fifteen years in the area of frontier holsters and gun belts. From near throw-away items kept only as accoutrements by a few Colt collectors, they became, by the mid-1970s, the focus of much attention, numerous articles, and extensive fakery. Even reference works have been permeated with out-and-out phonies.

In this climate, collectors have become more cautious. Demand remains high for maker-marked items that are well integrated and representative of their maker, but much obviously newly-stamped or upgraded stuff is around. While old catalogs are a help in recognizing items, a feel for old leather must also be developed by the collector. New items are easily aged.

There is increased interest lately in the Hollywood, or *Buscadero*, style holster rigs by prominent makers, but most collectors prefer the older frontier-style items. Most shun snaps, zippers, aluminum, or late tooling styles, but, unlike gun collectors, don't seem to mind bunkhouse improvements of nickel spots, conchos, ranch brands, and 'dobe dollars, if contemporary to the item's use.

It helps in dating leather to know that snaps and tubular rivets are turn-of-the-century items, that two-piece, copper-washer-style rivets began early but are still on the market, and that most early gunbelt buckles were rectangular, unplated, and cast. The clip-cornered California or garrison buckles came later. Early nickel spots are plated brass, not steel, and some makers continued to use territorial stamps for years after their states were annexed.

(SEE BELTS, SADDLE SCABBARDS)

160) Though early percussion holsters often hung from the pommels of military saddles, these two *cantanas*, or pommel bag holsters, were for the civilian trade. The left one, by *W.L. Pickard & Son, Salt Lake City*, holds a Colt single-action. The right is by *Main & Winchester, San Francisco* and holds a pocket model.

161) Full-flap holsters for the huge Dragoon Colt, dimunitive New Line, and the 1851 Navy Belt pistol. The Dragoon holster has been tarred, an early method of water-proofing leather. The button-flapped Navy holster was used by Utah gunman William A. Hickman.

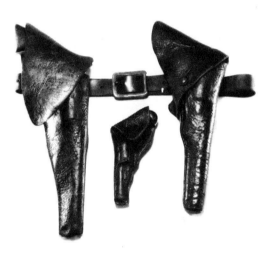

162) A fine *Lanz, Owen & Co., Chicago* Model 1885 U.S. Cavalry holster for both the Colt and Smith and Wesson revolvers on the rare Anson Mills model 1880 cartridge belt. Early U.S. military holsters are "left hand draw," and numerous civilian ones follow the military style.

163) Three nice percussion-era civilian California or Slim Jim open-top holsters. Note the vine-style floral carving, sewn-in toe plug, and close-fitting contours. The belts are a police, a civilian, and a Benicia Arsenal-marked U.S. Model 1874 sabre belt.

164) An early, closely-contoured Mexican double-loop holster with the classic edge-embossing and a single large rosette. This holster was fully lined. The 32.20 caliber combination money and cartridge belt is marked *J.S. Collins & Co., Cheyenne, Wyo.*

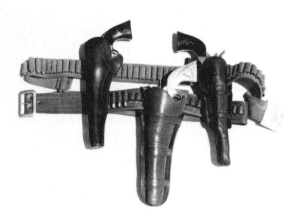

165) Three early 71/2" Colt single-action holsters. An edge-tooled Slim Jim. A three-looped, Mexican *Merwin and Bray* red felt-lined holster. A short-flapped, double Mexican loop custom-made for Utah rancher K. McClure in the 1890s.

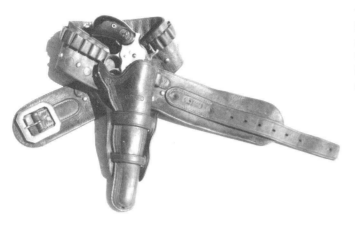

166) Probably the most popular of all gun leather names, F.A. Meanea of Cheyenne, made this 71/2" holster and its 31/2" wide cartridge and money belt. This holster is unusual in that it lacks the sewn-in *Cheyenne toe* typical of Meanea holsters.

167) The cowboys' big five calibers are represented by these old money-belt rigs in 32.20, 38.40, .41 Colt, 44.40, and .45 Colt. The top belt is stamped *C.W. Bell* a previous owner. The second is a mail-order *Rival* that has some home decoration. The center is a high quality *M.E. French, Montrose, Colo.* Fourth is a typical Texas *jock-strap* holster on mail-order belt, and finally a Sears best-quality holster on homemade money belt.

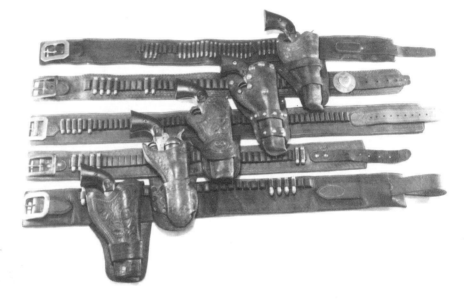

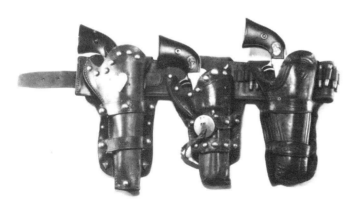

168) Holsters by Montgomery Ward, left, and Rival, center, are probably helped by the genuinely old addition of nickel spots and conchos, but the fine early *S.C. Gallup and Frazier* holster has been seriously damaged by having been shortened.

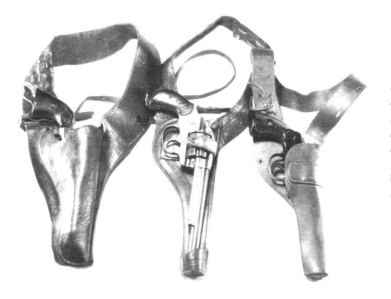

169) Shoulder holsters date even earlier than the Western frontier, and the use of the Texas pouch-type, like the unmarked example at left, was popular with Old West gunmen. This speed-draw, skeleton spring clip style, center, was made by Al Furstnow, Miles City, Montana. The half-breed at right made by Visalia Stock Saddle Co. was an even later item.

170) These two Colt Lightning revolvers are in lightweight, machine-embossed, mass-manufactured holsters often referred to as mail-order items. At left is a double Mexican loop, and at right is a simple pouch-style with its original 60¢ price penciled on the back.

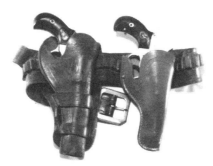

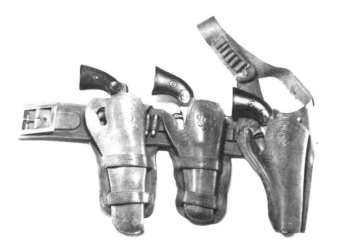

171) The occurrence of rather attractive edge and rosette-embossed holsters marked only with model numbers and the words *Olive* or *Olive Patent* is not uncommon. This very similarly machine-stamped shoulder holster has the famous diamond brand of the Shapleigh Hardware Co., which may suggest their origin.

172) This early snub-nosed revolver, a Colt Model 1889, is being carried in a plain mail-order holster on a worn *J.A. Donnel, Rawlins, Wyoming* .41 caliber combination money and cartridge belt. Because maker names add value and interest to belts and holsters, many marks are now being faked.

173) A major maker of quality gun leather for many years, the Herman H. Heiser Co., Denver, continued operation into the 1950s. These three holsters are typical of their diverse line.

174) All five of these items are marked *Browning Bros., Ogden, Utah* but were actually manufactured by H.H. Heiser at Denver. The family of the famous firearms inventor, John Browning, ran a large retail and wholesale sporting-goods business until after his death in 1926.

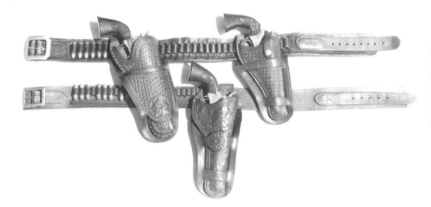

175) The .45 caliber R.T. Frazier combination belt at top has a black body but russet leather billets. It would have sold with the holster at left for $4.75 in 1927. The matched rig below is marked *White & Davis, Always Reliable, Pueblo, Colo.*, but was manufactured by Heiser.

176) Though unmarked, the top rig is recognizable from old catalogs as Sears' *Cowboy Combined Cartridge and Money Belt* and *Handcarved Mexican Style Cowboy Holster*. Bottom, a pre-war matched rig by the George Lawrence Co., Portland, one of the last of the old quality makers to stop production.

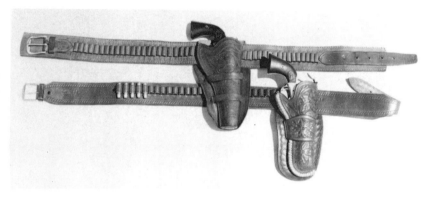

177) Though most of the West's saddlers were respected and sometimes influential businessmen, Bob Meldrum was a feared and hated hired gun. Reputedly the killer of fifteen men, usually under the sanction of a badge, "Bad Man" Meldrum was finally convicted of manslaughter for a killing while he was marshal of Baggs, Wyoming. He was sent to Wyoming State Prison at Rawlins, where he made this holster.

178) This *Farley and Frank, the Dalles, Oregon* holster for a 51/2" single-action Colt on a Mills *dog head* 32-20 caliber belt is still getting occasional use in the hills near Meeker, Colorado. Using old equipment is a part of the joy of collecting it.

179) One of the few authentic fast-draw rigs of the Old West, the *Bridgeport* is a rare and frequently-phonied item. The revolver is hung by the extended hammer screw in the belt-mounted clip. This one is stamped *PAT'D JAN. 17, 1882* and *BRIDGEPORT, G.I. CO.* on the plate fingers. It is mounted with round-headed, copper, two-piece rivets on a money combination belt marked *J.S. Collins, Cheyenne.*

180) The Phillipine heritage of this U.S. Model 1896 Colt is obvious from its black civilian holster marked *Maestranza De Manila.* The belt is by Fred Mueller, Denver, Colorado.

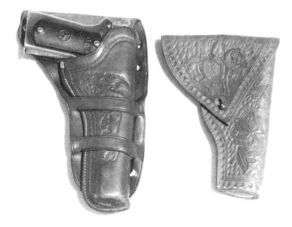

181) Most collector interest wanes in the age of automatics, but this Mexican loop holster for the 1902 Colt Auto has an alluring art nouveau maiden embossed, and the 1903 Auto holster has a carved cowboy motif.

182) Three small hip-pocket revolver holsters. The first has a safety spring over the trigger guard and a magazine for cartridges. It was patented July 17, 1900. The center is marked *Diamond Brand*, and the one at the far right has cartridge loops.

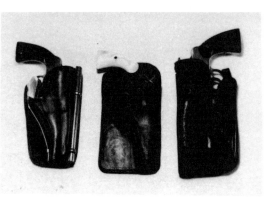

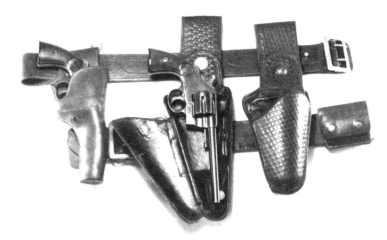

183) Patent holsters that find some interest with collectors include the Audley, patented October 13, 1914, which featured a spring-operated trigger-guard-locking device. The larger, spring-open *Clam Shell* holster was made by C.A. Hoffman & Son, and the smaller one was made by Stanroy Manufacturing Co.

HAND CUFFS

Another accoutrement associated with the Old West lawmen were the handcuffs they carried. Certain types were popular in the western territories, but others like the currently imported English Darby style were virtually unknown.

A few specialized collectors will pay substantial sums for rare handcuffs, leg irons and other restraints, but most collectors are interested only in the few items related to law enforcement in the Wild West.

184) At the top are a pair of early Tower single-lock barrel key handcuffs, popular after the Civil War in the West. Below is a pair of Bean/Cobb improved handcuffs patented in 1899.

HATS

An old cowboy legend tells of John B. Stetson wandering through the West, sick, broke, and unemployed. He saw early Westerners dig a hole and press a wet hide down it with a post to produce a hat. Right off, he invented the felt cowboy hat, got rich and healthy, and lived to a ripe old age.

Actually, the illustrious John B. was the frail son of a New Jersey master hatter who did indeed come west to Missouri prior to the Civil War. Realizing a need and market for better quality felt hats, he set up business in Philadelphia and began manufacture of his famous *Boss of the PLains*. His success is shown by the fact that his name had become synonymous with cowboy hats by the time he died in 1906.

Early California vaqueros preferred low, flat-crowned, and brimmed felt hats with tie strings but later adopted the Yankee Stetsons. Plainsmen usually wore the cavalry-style slouch hats with somewhat floppy brims, or the flat-crowned, Southern-planter style. By the 1880s, style-conscious cowboys all wore cowboy hats, and after the turn-of-the-century, the rodeo and movie influence took them to extremes.

Collectors will find that nice old hats, like boots, were expendable and are now scarce. The majority are not Stetson make, as the Philadelphia outfit always had lots of competition. Many post-1900 hats will have no maker's name only the name of the retail outlet that sold them. Finally, the various crown creases and brim styles have distinct regional significance until about 1915, when the movies set more universal styles.

185) Left is the very wide-brimmed plainsman hat made famous by such showmen as Buffalo Bill. Right, the extremely high-crowned ten-gallon hat of the movie era. Sears cataloged this *Bond Street DeLuxe—Big Boy* for $4.95 in 1927.

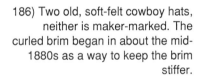

186) Two old, soft-felt cowboy hats, neither is maker-marked. The curled brim began in about the mid-1880s as a way to keep the brim stiffer.

187) The Mexican sombrero, left, is one ancestor of the cowboy hat. Various states of Mexico have different styles. Black has always been a popular color in Stetsons, for good guys or bad.

188) Hat crease and styles have been subject to regional and time variations. The Stetson at left has wide band and raw-edge brim, the one at right, narrow band and bound edge.

189) This nice, old Stetson and its hand-hitched horsehair band have been preserved in nearly new condition since they were sold in 1934 at Safford, Arizona.

190) Most expensive of all Stetsons, the huge *Tom Mix* featured 7 1/2" crown and 5 1/2" curled brim and took well over half a month of a cowboy's pay in the 1920s.

191) From the left, a late but prominent competitor in fine felt hats is Resistol. This old Stetson is a campaign hat, standard with doughboys and border-patrol men but scoffed at by cowboys as a "Boy Scout" hat. Another early, soft-felt hat by Merrimac.

HOBBLES

Hobbles were the devices used to tie together a horse's front legs or, less frequently, a front and rear leg. Most were buckled leather cuffs with a short chain between or a length of leather with a ring situated to permit buckling it in a figure-eight configuration. Some were made of braided leather or rawhide, often using Turks' heads as fasteners.

One intriguing all-iron type is called the *Mormon* or *trick* hobble. Tradition has it that Indians had great difficulty solving the Chinese-puzzle-type opening system and were, therefore, unable to steal horses thus hobbled. Though these really were used in the Old West, they are popularly reproduced. Look for authentic wear and hand-forged parts.

Though real cowboys often hobbled their horses with their sashes, bandannas, or even gunnysacks, collectors will likely find more interest in fine quality braided hobbles or those with the cartouche of desirable makers.

192) Pictured is a pair of very ordinary chain and leather hobbles with a swiveling center link.

193) This pair of *Mormon* hobbles is hand-wrought of iron. There is a trick to opening and separating the cuffs which, according to the lore, kept horses safer from marauding Indians.

KNIVES

Certainly any knife available might well have been used by cowboys, but certain types are most identified with them. Early travelers often noted the wearing of large sheath knives at the belt, and old photos of cowboys and Texas Rangers show them displayed prominently. These knives, or dirks, were late remnants of the great Bowie-knife tradition, which was extant in the whole United States but most particularly the South and Southwest from the 1820s to well after the Civil War.

The Bowie knife, a true sidearm, might be any of several early styles—clip-point, spear-point, or double-edged. Careful researchers conclude that the legendary Jim Bowie actually used a knife resembling a large French chef's knife. Early Bowie knives of American origin are valuable treasures, and their more common English counterparts only slightly less so. Many early Bowies reflect superb quality and decoration.

Early Bowie knives were distinctly weapons, but with increased reliance on the revolver as sidearm, the post-Civil War Bowie became increasingly a utilitarian tool. Plainer styling and slab, stag handles replaced silver, mother of pearl, and exotic woods. The distinction between Bowie knife and sheath hunting knife became moot.

Actually, true early hunting knives were rarely carried at the belt. The percussion-era hunter usually carried these utilitarian straight *Butcher* or curved skinning knives in his hunting or possibles bag. Though most of these were also imported from Sheffield, England, the most collectible for Westerners is the famous *Green River* of the J. Russel & Co. of Massachusetts. Cowboys, like their fur-hunting predecessors, used these hunting knives but kept them in their saddle bags or soogans.

Another cowboy knife with roots in the fur trade is the farriers' or hoof knife. These are later versions of the crooked knife often traded to Indians. Their bent-over blade ends are equally useful for fleshing hides or cleaning hooves. Most were shipped without handles from Sheffield. I*XL and other famous Bowie maker-marks are common.

Various styles of sheath hunting knives evolved in the mid- to latter 19th century. In England, the Shakespear knife, a design of Major Henry Shakespear, explorer, hunter, and author, met some success. As a grandaddy of the Syke Fairbairn Commando dagger, the big, double-edged Shakespear looks very much a weapon. In San Francisco, about 1870, another style was developed. Evolving from both the Bowie and Butcher knife eras, the California Camp knife has been called the first true American hunting knife. Strictly for sport, its sharpened false edge is for use as a hatchet on animal bone or sticks.

Concurrently and through the turn-of-the-century, England, Germany, and other European cutlers exported hunting knives generally styled after the Bowie tradition, though most often lighter, with narrower guards, and slab-stag or even deer-foot handles. After the turn-of-the-century, American makers evolved the more typical and modern-appearing sports hunting knife. All, of course, were used by cowboys.

They also used virtually any type of pocketknife, but the large jackknives take precedence with collectors. The large Horseman's knife, distinguished by its hoof pick or hook is a tool designed for utility. Like so many cowboy knives, it has Anglo ancestry.

194) Early sheath knives include (left) a large fullered and double-edged hunting knife developed by mid-19th century adventurer, Maj. Henry Shakespear. Its sheath is leather-covered wood with a release clip. The knife is marked *Shakespear Knife* and *Wilkinson, London.* Center is a true spear-point Bowie knife, circa 1855. Its thick blade is marked *Booth, Norfolk Works, Sheffield.* The guard at the hilt has been altered and its sheath is a later replacement. Virtually all British bowies were shipped with light leather, part metal sheaths. To the right is a late (post 1880) style Bowie marked *LF & C.* Though it retains a very heavy blade and wide-style hilt and guard, it has a handle that tapers toward the butt, a mark of later Bowie-style hunting knives. The sheath is Sioux beaded, circa 1900.

195) The California Camp or hunting knife, top, is a scarce variation of the 1870s. This one is rosewood-handled and marked *Will & Finck, S.F. Cal.* Below it is a curved skinning knife stamped *J. Russell & Co., Green River Works.* The diamond in the deep-stamped trademark indicates manufacture after 1875. Left, another essential of cowboy cutlery, the straight razor, was left in his poke, rolled in his soogan or war bag. This fancy stork-handled one is marked *Oxford Cutlery Co. Germany.* Third from the top is a hoof or farriers' knife with a simple, slotted, antler-handle. It is marked *I*XL, G. Wostenholm & Sons, Washington Works, Sheffield* a famous Bowie-knife maker. Bottom is a campers' knife and fork, which slide into their respective handles, marked on the side *Eden Hotel Rome.*

196) From the left are a clip-point, Bowie-style hunting knife, a spear-point, and another clip-point showing substantial wear. All three are marked *Non-XLL, Joseph Allen & Sons, Sheffield, England.* The presence of the country name indicates manufacture after 1890. The knives are of lighter, thinner steel than most true bowies, have thinner hilt guards, and have the tapered handle styles that help date them. The knife to the right is a traditional, double-edge dagger of pre-1890 vintage marked *H. York-Sheffield.*

197) A variety of sheath knives. Left, a single-edge dirk or hunting knife marked *Roslers Nachfolger Austria*. Similar turn-of-the-century imports often have deer-foot handles. A hunting knife by famous *J. Russell & Co., Green River Works* has a serrated blade back for scaling fish and a sharpened false edge at its clip point. Right, this unmarked, nice quality dagger appears to be North European. The top part of its metal-and-leather sheath is gone.

198) The knife at the top is probably the last style of true Bowie knives. Its thick blade is stamped *John Bull, Sheffield*. The full tang and stag handles do not taper, and it has a heavy, stepped, German silver guard. It is believed to have been used at Aspen, Colorado, in the early 1880s. The second knife is unmarked, probably American, and has a stylish tooled sheath. Though it has a thick blade and stepped guard, it does show the transitional tapered handle-line of evolving hunting knife styles. The third knife is a very large, clip-blade, Bowie-style knife marked *W. Clauberg - Est. 1810, Solingen, Germany*. Imported German knives almost all date after 1885, later than the true Bowie era, and most, like this one, are after WW I. Quality can be very good, but collector appeal lags. The bottom knife, marked *Remington - UMC*, is typical of myriad American-manufactured hunting knives from several makers after about 1900. Many have stacked leather handles, and values depend greatly on brand and condition. Sheathes with snap closures are post-1900.

199) Large, folding jackknives are perhaps more popular with collectors than they were even with cowboys. Differentiated from sheath, or fixed-blade knives, these too were sometimes worn folded in belt sheathes. From the left, a horseman's knife with hoof pick, corkscrew, and leather punch marked *Chornhill, London*. A large, desirable pre-1900 folder marked *New York Knife Co., Walden, Hammer Brand*. An early, patented folder from *Marbles Safety Axe Co*. Another large, swell-center folding jack with celluloid handles marked *Colonial-Providence*. Finally, a canoe-style, folding hunter marked *Case-Tested XX*. All of these knives are more than five inches long closed, and values are very dependent on maker names and condition.

LOADING TOOLS

Like other frontiersmen, the cowboys circumstances behooved them to reload their cartridges. The remoteness of sources and the expense and bulk of loaded ammunition made it prohibitive for the man who used much of it. So, like the buffalo hunters before him, the cowboy usually chose to "roll his own."

In black-powder days, the process was especially simple. The empty cartridge case was its own powder measure. It was reprimed and filled to the top. A purchased or cast bullet was seated over it, and the case was crimped with the appropriate loading tool. Often this was even further simplified by the fact that some cowboys used the same cartridge—.44, .38, .32 Winchester—in both their rifles and revolvers. One size, one gun belt, and one loading tool!

The advent of smokeless powders in the 1890s began to complicate hand loading. The new powders were more difficult to use, requiring careful measure or weighing. Most frontiersmen simply continued to use the old black powder for reloading, but some, of course, learned the new techniques.

Collectors are showing increased interest in old loading tools. Many gun manufacturers began to offer these in the 1870s, and the Bridgeport Gun Implement Co. and Ideal Manufacturing Co. specialized in them. The varieties and calibers are virtually limitless.

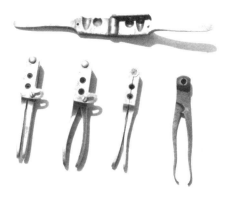

200) Early bullet molds from the percussion era include very early Colt dragoon mold (top), various other Colt molds and old percussion-rifle, round-ball mold.

201) From the left, a Winchester bullet-mold and the Model 1882 loading tool in .44 W.C.F. Caliber and a .32-165 mold and Model 1894 loading tool. The designation for most black-powder cartridges like .32-40-165 gives caliber, weight of powder charge, and weight of bullet.

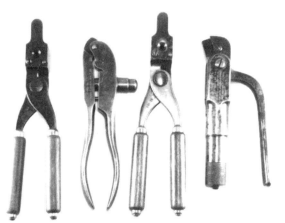

202) Though frontiersmen could and sometimes did buy factory-made bullets for reloading, many chose to cast their own from lead or lead alloys. A small, cast-iron lead pot was then a necessity.

203) The advent of smokeless powders required more care and sophistication in measurement. This early Fairbanks scale measures in grains and is part of an early reloading kit.

204) Shotgunners, too, reloaded their cases. These tools deprime, reprime, cut wads, and re-crimp the then-new paper cases. Some brass ones are in the old loading block. Several tools are marked B.G.I. Co.

NECKERCHIEFS

Known variously as bandannas, kerchiefs, scarves, or wild rags, the cowboy's use of the neckerchief has endured since his beginning. Essentially a large handkerchief, its uses seem nearly endless. They range from protection of the neck or face from weather and dust to hog-tying calves and blindfolding broncs. The neckerchief was his towel, his ear muffs, and, with some errant few, a mask.

Early neckerchiefs were often of heavy silk and were, just as today, expensive. Cheaper work-a-day substitutes were the brightly-hued, dyed-cotton kerchiefs of the South and of Mexico. Movie influences developed the huge bandannas of the 'teens and 1920s, which were often worn with a slide. By the 1920s and 1930s, most major rodeos and numerous saddle catalogs had souvenir silk scarves emulating Pendleton's *Let 'er Buck* motif.

206) A bright red, paisley-like pattern, this neckerchief is typical of those from Mexico used throughout the plains. Being of unsanforized cotton, it has shrunk out of square.

205) This very early, pure purple silk neckerchief was worn by a central Utah rancher while chasing Indians on militia duty. Though frayed, it remains serviceable.

207) This bright silk scarf was a souvenir of Ogden Pioneer Days rodeo of 1935. A leather neckerchief slide with a steer head can be seen at the left. Similar bright scarves were mail-ordered by most large saddlery outfitters.

208) A cheap, cotton, triangular neckerchief was printed with a Pioneer Days motif. This souvenir item was made for youngsters and sold at rodeos and parades.

POKES

Scarce and often over-looked by collectors are those medium to small buckskin bags in which cowboys kept their treasures. The poke was usually kept in the war bag or bedroll and might contain shaving gear, a picture of a sweetheart, or a letter from home.

Many early cowboys carried all of their money, usually in hard coin, inside of their gunbelts, but some might also carry a poke, especially when gold dust was used as specie, securely tied by its drawstrings, somewhere on their person. Horseback riding makes anything carried in the pockets very subject to loss.

Many of these early pokes were made by reservation Indians. As with the beaded gauntlet gloves, cowboys were among their best customers for fancy decorated buckskin bags.

209) This early, beaded buckskin poke has the usual drawstring top closure and a dangler of trade beads. It is believed to have been Apache made. Both sides have the scatter beads and Christian cross designs.

POWDER FLASKS AND HORNS

Though the heyday of the Western cowboy was in the cartridge era, his roots spring from the percussion-gun era. Indeed, many drovers continued to carry old cap-and-ball firearms well into the 1880s.

Flask and powder horn collecting are themselves a wide field of interest, both as accoutrements to flint- and percussion-era firearms and for their own sake. Cowboy collectors are likely to be most interested in those related to old Colt revolvers or with some linkage to Western history.

210) The large but plain powder horn at top was used in the defense of Fort Limhi, Salmon, Idaho in 1857. The flasks include a U.S. military "peace" flask, a brass sporting-scene flask, and a similar scene pressed in leather. The final leather flask was used for shot.

QUIRTS

Once the veritable badge of the Plains cowboy, quirts (from the Spanish *cuerda*) remain popular only with collectors. These short, flexible whips often reflect beautiful rawhide or leather braiding, and a few, those mostly for show, are even hitched of horsehair.

Quirts commonly have a thong or whang leather loop or wrist band fastened to the braided body. The body may be braided leather or rawhide over a core of leather or sometimes buckshot or metal. This weight at the top end makes such a quirt an effective blackjack. At the bottom is a folded leather strip called a lash or popper. The romal, which emanates from the Californio's reins, is a lightweight quirt.

Collectors are most interested in quirts that show fine workmanship and age.

211) From the left: This light wood-core quirt is made from hitched horsehair, and it likely originated in a Western prison. The skirting of hair or leather on some quirts is called *frills*. A contemporary, rawhide quirt braided in Mexico. Center: This old Hamley quirt was ordered by the late Charles Guild in 1930. It is braided rawhide with 6 Turks'-head buttons. This finely-braided leather quirt reflects exceptional quality. Right: plainer, this old quirt has coarser cut and braid.

REINS

Like bits and bridles, the cowboy's reins reflect traditional differences between horse gear west and east of the Rocky Mountains. The California vaquero's bit had chains that attached to his closed reins, which in turn attached to a light whip extension called the romal. These reins and romal were often handsomely braided rawhide or leather.

The Texan or plainsman, on the other hand, dropped his open or split reins when he dismounted. They were most often of plain leather and attached directly to the lower rings of his curb bit. Occasionally, these split reins, too, were made of braided rawhide or leather, and were usually tapered and about seven feet long.

Collectors are usually most interested in the elaborate California reins. The 1934 Visalia Catalog shows fancy braided California rein and romal sets from 4 to 16 plait, with as many as eighty braided Turk's Heads, and priced from $3 to $12.50

(SEE BITS, BRIDLES)

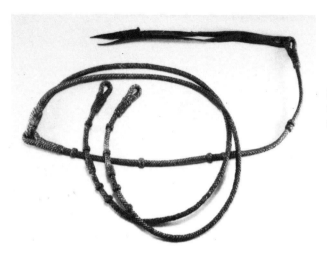

212) A set of California-style reins and romal braided of rawhide. This set is only of average quality for older reins.

213) A modern set of California reins and romal braided of leather. It does not have the quality and style of older pieces.

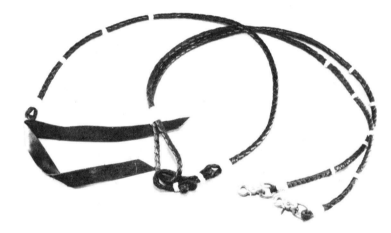

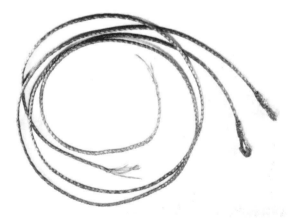

214) A set of braided rawhide reins of split or open style. These are of simple 4-plait braiding, but are well done.

ROPES AND REATAS

The one item of cowboy gear that would seem distinctly American in origin is the lariat or *la reata*. Originating in Mexico, the lariat made possible the handling of half-wild cattle in the vast, unfenced West. Without it, American-style ranching and the cowboy could not have existed. Indeed, the lariat combined with the horned saddle creates the most intrinsic difference between cowboys and the rest of history's mounted herdsmen.

As with much other cowboy gear, ropes west and east of the Rockies developed distinct differences. The California vaquero used a very long, 60- to 80-foot, rawhide reata and took twists or *dallys* around his horn. His Texas cowboy contemporary, on the other hand, usually used a rope 30 to 40 feet long, which he tied fast to his saddle horn.

Among collectors, the beautifully braided, rawhide reatas get obvious preference. Some are true works of art and skilled *reateros* were among the finest of Old California craftsmen. Rawhide reatas and dally-roping spread north and east with the vaquero style.

Grass ropes, those made of maguey, hemp, flax, sisal, or other vegetable fibres are less valued by collectors. They are usually thirty to forty feet long and are tightly twisted. Originally handmade, lengths of hard twist *whale line* quickly became a general-store item in Texas and the Plains. Small patent machines for twisting rope are also found and collected.

Another rope originating in California but ultimately found everywhere in the West is the *mecate* or McCarty. Usually of twisted horsehair, they average about twenty-two feet long. They were used in Mexico and California to tie the horse, rig out the hackamore, and decorate the big alamar knot around the horse's neck. One bit of cowboy lore claims that if horsehair ropes were laid around his bed, rattlesnakes would not cross them.

215) *La reata larga*, or long rope, of Mexico is braided rawhide. The working vaquero or arena *charro* piles coils of rope on the pommel of his saddle and takes dallys or twists when he ropes. This one is 4-plait and about 70 feet long.

216) An 80-foot braided rawhide reata of American style. Probably made in Oregon, it was the proud possession of the late Wallace Irwin, Y Cross Ranch, Cheyenne, Wyoming.

217) A very light 3/8" reata has a Mexican-style revolving honda. Reata ropers gave lassoed animals play on the line rather than pulling down abruptly.

218) Another American reata used in Utah. Like most working reatas, it is made of four strands of untanned cowhide. Fancier ropes are six or sometimes eight strands.

219) A very nice and unusual reata, this forty-footer is thicker, stronger, and could be tied hard. It originated in northwest Colorado.

220) A nice, old, mane-hair rope in black and white, this twenty-two-foot McCarty was twisted by the late Joe Roberts, Maybell, Colorado, in the winter of 1930.

221) Another twenty-two-foot McCarty from the Spanish *mecate*, this well-made, all-black rope saw use in Utah.

222) An interesting accoutrement of the later competitive arena ropers is the rope bag or box. This extensively tooled leather one was the proud possession of rodeo cowboy Tex Austin Jr.

SADDLES

From the decades of Santa Fe trade, well before the Civil War, stockmen of Texas and California had spurned the light saddles of the East, preferring instead the heavy, thick-horned Mexican saddle. Indeed, it was the horned saddle, along with another Mexican invention, the *reata*, that would make possible the American cattle industry, which was based on handling stock on open ranges.

By trail-driving days, Texans had evolved their own variations of stock saddles. They added a rear cinch to the front-rigged, Spanish style, fleshed the saddle out with square fenders or sometimes attached the old removable Mexican *mochila* or covering, and called it "Mother Hubbard."

In the later 1860s and 1870s, the Texas trail would widen and deepen by Pueblo, Denver, and on to Cheyenne. There, along the trail, the most notable of the Plains cowboy saddle-makers developed: Heiser, Frazier, Gallatin, Gallup, Meanea, and the Collins brothers.

In California, a separate tradition developed. The vaquero had adopted the Indian's single, or center-fire, rig by 1860, the Easterner's bentwood stirrups to which he added long tapaderos by the 1870s, and finally the high-horned, famous Visalia tree by 1880. Through her numerous famous saddlers, Main and Winchester, Stone, Shuham and Walker among them, California developed her own reputation and, ultimately, a collectors' tradition.

As with other gear, the California styles moved north to Oregon and east to the Rockies. As the vaquero became the buckaroo, his high-horned, round-skirted saddle became hybridized with the Plains style. By the turn-of-the-century, makers from most areas were making saddles of all styles, and the regional distinctions began to blur.

Collectors of cowboy saddles seem primarily interested in maker-marked saddles of pre-1900 origin. Originality and condition are important, and, though careful restoration is encouraged, repairs not well blended in seem offensive. Major remodeling such as rounding off the old square skirts is downright sinful!

Though most of the saddles about which I receive calls are always "a hundred years old," dating the origins of certain saddle styles is not difficult. The large, low-horned Mother Hubbard was the standard of the 1870s. The big, square-skirted, Plains saddle replaced it in the early 1880s, and most of these began to sport separate seat jockeys by 1885. Loop seats predominate in the 1890s from California to Montana, and any saddle with swells, slick horn, extra high cantle, or deep *Pueblo* seat can be pretty safely dated into this century. Note that this only dates beginnings; a saddle of very early style may have been made last month.

223) Typical of the early, cheap, trail saddles, this worn, old, wood-horn has outside Sam Stagg double rigging, 131/2" seat, a low 21/2" cantle, and bentwood *doghouse* stirrups on narrow leathers. The Cheyenne roll cantle probably dates it into the 1880s.

224) Its *G.H. & J.S. Collins, Cheyenne* stamp at the mochila corners date this early Mother Hubbard between 1876 and 1880. It has double rig, 15" seat, 41/2" plain cantle, 31/2" high and wide horn, and the mochila or macheer is 15" x 29" to the side.

225) A classic "forty dollar" saddle, this 1885 *S.C. Gallup, Pueblo, Col.*, 151/2" half-seat features a unique style of Sam Stagg rigging, side jockeys, 33/4" Cheyenne roll cantle, and 21/2" high by 4" wide horn. The square skirts are 141/2" x 271/2".

226) The California influence is obvious in this 1880s *Jenkins & Sons* (Salt Lake City) 15" cowboy saddle with its higher 5" cantle and 4" high and wide horn. It has plains-style, Sam Stagg, double rigging in which the back rings are secured by the rear jockeys.

227) This *Marks Bros. Saddle Co. Omaha, Neb.* marked, lighter, stock saddle is a 15" half-seat with separate jockeys, 33/4" Cheyenne roll cantle, and it has a 3" slanted horn on its "Warranted Steel Fork." The square skirts measure 121/2" x 24". Note the added bucking roll on this early 1890s rig.

228) The 14 P *F.A. Meanea, Cheyenne, W.T.* may have been the most common of Northern Plains saddles of the 1890s. This one has 17" seat, 5" plain cantle, 4" high horn, and 14" x 29" skirts. Loop seats were standard until after the turn of the century, when full seats (without the visible stirrup leathers) became more common.

229) *R.T. Frazier, Pueblo, Colo* saddle #196 is a very heavy rig with its 16" seat, 51/2" Cheyenne roll cantle, 3" silver horn, large 16" x 31" skirts, and matched saddle pockets. It features combined floral and basket-weave tooling and a variety of Frazier stamps. It dates about 1900.

230) A classic *Pueblo*, this slightly-later-styled *R.T. Frazier* #187 has a more concave 51/2" fancy rope-bound cantle, 16" seat, 3" brass horn with all brass trimmings, 16" x 28" skirts, and is full-floral tooled. These nicer "forty dollar saddles" were more than twice that by the 'teens.

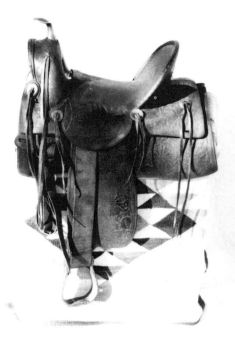

231) This special-order #142 *R.T. Frazier* saddle has an early-style, exposed Sam Stagg front rigging, 141/2" seat, 41/2" Cheyenne roll cantle with the initials *V.B.C.* on the back, 3" leather-covered horn, ribbon and basket-weave tooling, the fanciest Frazier stirrups, and some silver conchos. The big old Mexican peso 'dobe dollars were likely added later.

232) This lady's astride saddle, in exceptionally fine condition, is marked *J.G. Harris, Greeley, Colorado.* It has a half seat with side jockeys but inside single rigging. Its seat measures 141/2", 5" plain cantle, 3" leather-covered horn, 12" x 24" skirts, narrow 2" stirrup leathers, and no provision for carrying a rope.

233) A later, post-1900 Mother Hubbard by *W.R. Thompson, Rifle, Colorado* features double rigging, 15" seat, 41/2" cantle, 3" high horn, and large mochila, 16" x 32" to the side. These iron-ring stirrups were popular in the 'teens, and Mother Hubbard saddles maintained some popularity in western Colorado and eastern Utah until about that era.

234) This *T. Flynn, Pueblo, Colo* marked #170 saddle has double rig, 15" seat, 51/2" cantle, 21/2" leather horn, 15" x 27" square skirts, and exceptionally nice condition. One stirrup fender has a burned ranch brand. The stirrups are ox bows bound with galvanized steel, probably the most common on post-1900 saddles.

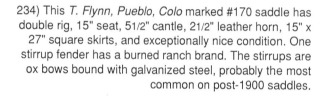

235) Special-ordered without a horn, this *R.T. Frazier* has a four-digit number *(2442)* and the large round *Pueblo* stamp on its cantle. Both seem to be indicative that it dates later than about 1920. It has a big 18" seat and 17" x 30" skirts with a single 7/8 rig. Hornless work saddles are sometimes called *muleys* and are scarce.

236) This large, old, stock saddle was made by the firm of *Collins and Morrison, Omaha Nebraska.* The large swells date it after the turn-of-the-century and probably around the time of the death of the firm's founder, J.S. Collins, in 1910.

237) A saddle type sometimes found on Western ranches, but with Eastern heritage, is the plantation saddle. It is seen with or without saddle horn.

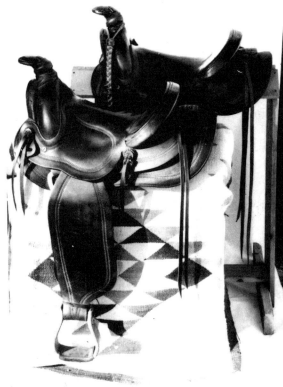

238) This matched pair of 1930s *J.M. Capriola, Elko, Nev.* saddles are serial numbered *0248* and *0249*. They have the California-influenced single 3/4 rig and rounded skirts but low Cheyenne roll cantles. They have 14" and 15" seats and were owned by the author's parents. Note that stirrup leathers were often integrated with the fenders by the 1930s.

239) "What's an old McClellan saddle worth?" is my second most frequently asked question (behind "Why did cowboys wear cuffs?".) This fine condition 12" russet RIA 1904 model has original rigging and horsehair girth and U.S. embossed covered-wood stirrups. It was acquired at a well-attended ranch auction for $80. Earlier, usually black-colored models go substantially higher.

SADDLE BAGS

Related of course to saddles, but also found separately, saddle bags or pockets are a very collectible miscellaneous item. Most are constructed of individual pockets that hang to each side of the saddle behind the cantle. Some, called *cantanas* or pommel bags, fit over the horn at the front of the saddle. Either style may be tooled extensively, covered with wool, patent leather, angora, or other hides, or marked by famous and collectible makers.

Favorites with collectors seem to be the bags with long angora goat hair and those with a stiff, long, outer flap cover, especially if maker-marked. Other fairly common items are the U.S. embossed saddle bags, especially the 1904 vintage russet leather style with canvas liners. Thousands of these were bought surplus after World War II, and they remain popular with military collectors and users.

Another item of some interest are the small staple pockets and fencing tool or other miscellaneous tool scabbards that are designed to tie in at string conchos or behind the cantleback. These were cataloged by most saddle makers, and famous names may have value.

(SEE GUN RIGS, SADDLES)

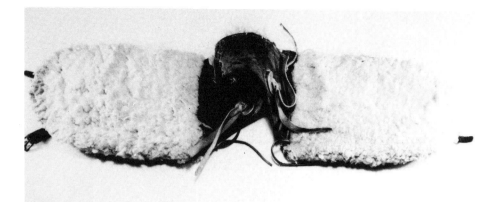

240) This hard-used, old pair of saddle pockets has the stiff flap type of covers that have been covered with sheepskin.

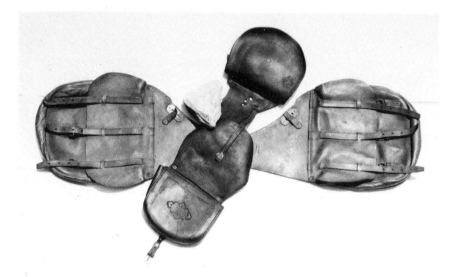

241) This old pair of small saddle pockets was made by Geo. C. Wilson, Delta, Colo. Maker marks add interest to most old leather gear. Like the McClellan saddles that they fit, Model 1904 saddle bags turn up everywhere. Collectors are fussy that they not be cut or altered, for example, cut so as to be tied with saddle strings. Users couldn't care less. Both like the canvas liners there.

242) These semi-modern saddle bags are larger and made by the Bona Allen Co. They usually hang on the author's using saddle.

SADDLE MAKER'S TOOLS

The tools employed by saddle and harness makers and repairmen have only recently come to the forefront as an adjunct of cowboy collectibles. Collected both because of their antique quality and functional usefulness, they remain moderately priced relative to newly manufactured items of similar quality.

Also collectible, the various old harness-stitching bench seats from either old saddle shops or U.S. Cavalry surplus are attractively decorative. Items belonging to or personally inscribed by famous old saddle makers, or, for that matter, bit-and-spur makers and other craftsmen, are especially collectible. Saddle-tool collectors will become very familiar with C.S. Osborne and Co., who have dominated the field since 1826.

243) Made, stamped, and used in the famous W.R. Thompson saddle shop in Rifle, Colorado, this quick gauge gave the width of harness leathers and traces quickly.

SADDLE SCABBARDS

The true saddle scabbard for rifle or carbine would seem a relatively recent innovation and is perhaps even a true cowboy invention. The mountain man and Indian had occasionally sheathed their percussion long guns in buckskin and tied them to their horses. The cavalryman used an abbreviated leather socket or boot along with a sling and snap to secure his carbine until the late 1890s. The cowboy, on the other hand, was using a full leather scabbard at least by the 1870s.

These early saddle scabbards show marked similarities to their contemporary, Slim Jim revolver holsters. They are slim-fitting, copper-riveted, and often show the floral, vine, and corner rosette carving patterns of the California holsters. They frequently have the sewn-in muzzle plug, which collectors call a Cheyenne toe.

Through the 1880s and 1890s, a blunter, fuller, less form-fitting style of scabbard began to predominate. Toes are usually sewn round and are amply wide to house the full underbarrel magazine popular on saddle guns of the era. Simple line or chain edge embossing styles predominate, and most, like their contemporary revolver holsters, are not maker-marked. The majority were manufactured in large plants for the flourishing mail-order and hardware jobber trade and will fit a variety of models.

Collectors seldom show quite the enthusiasm for old scabbards that they do for belt holsters. Interest is primarily focused on the early, Slim Jim type or nice quality scabbards with well-known maker-names. Caution must be exercised, as with all leather collectibles, that these collectible names are not just recently-stamped phonies.

(SEE GUN RIGS, WINCHESTERS)

244) This very early Model 1866 rifle scabbard (top) has the vine-and-leaf carving, corner rosettes, Cheyenne toe, copper rivets, and double curving lines of earliest Slim Jim revolver holsters. Its fragile condition reduces value to about the same as the later but finer example below.

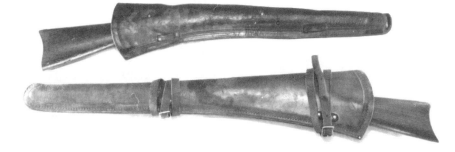

245) By the 1880s, scabbards usually show broader, blunter contours with a straighter seam and simpler edge embossing. Carbine scabbards for 20" barrels will average about 32" long. Rifles scabbards seem a bit more common in big-game areas, and those large enough for the big 1876 and 1886 Winchester rifles, 38" to 40", are especially desirable.

246) All three of these rifle scabbards are marked *Browning Bros. Ogden, Utah*. The famous inventor and his brothers were retail and wholesale dealers from the early 1880s until his death in 1926. Most Browning-marked gun leather originated in the shop of H.H. Heiser, Denver.

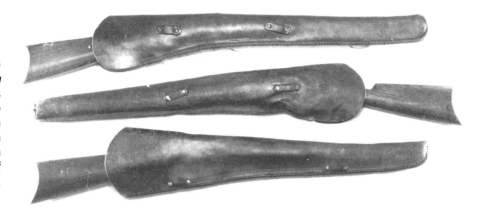

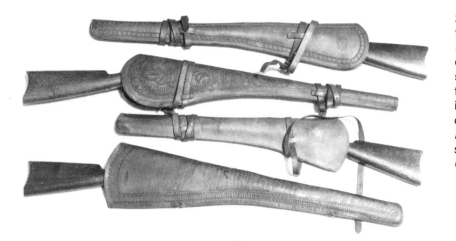

247) From the top, a border-tooled scabbard marked *Searle Saddlery, Vernal, Utah*; a contoured, hand-carved 1870s-style scabbard with Cheyenne toe, though its "patent" rivets indicate later manufacture; carbine scabbard by *Brauer Bros., St. Louis*; and a large rifle scabbard by *F.A. Meanea, Cheyenne.*

248) Though stamped Frank Bregenzer, Rifle, Colorado, the top scabbard appears to be a mass produced mail-order item. The semi-modern carbine scabbard at center is a Heiser #332. Bottom is *The Western Saddle Mfg. Co. Denver, Colo.* Hand edge-tooled scabbard #24, likely indicating the barrel length for which it is best suited.

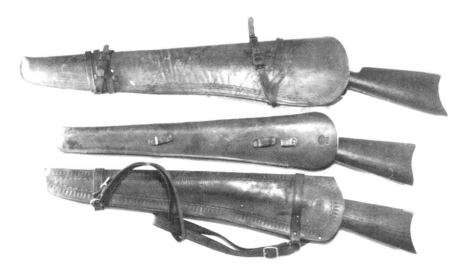

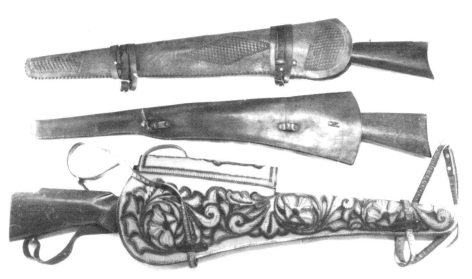

249) A basket-weave-stamped rifle scabbard by *Eubanks Leather, Boise, Idaho*; a plain, contoured rifle scabbard by *N.L. Blair, Pinedale, Wyoming*; and a very deeply carved, sheepskin-lined modern-scoped rifle scabbard produced by an inmate of Utah State Prison.

SCALES, TONGUE OR HIDER'S

The small hunter's scale has always been a favorite of Western-relic collectors. Though used variously as a sack scale or for other ranch purposes, the strongest association is with the professional hunters who used them to weigh buffalo tongues for marketing.

These are being copied currently, and the new ones have a brass calibration plate. Other collectible Western scales are the large steelyards and small gold-weighing scales.

(SEE LOADING TOOLS)

250) The small tongue scale was two scales in one. Either the large or small ring and hook could be used, depending on the size of the object to be weighed. These are usually entirely hand-wrought.

SKIRTS, RIDING

Virtually from the beginning of the cowboy era, some girls were cowboying, too. By the close of the nineteenth century, women in the West began to spurn the side-saddle and adopt the astride style of riding. Ladies' astride saddles became regular catalog items, and the split riding-skirt evolved.

Basically culottes, most of the everyday items were made of heavy cotton and had a buttoned panel in front that disguised the split legs. More durable skirts of leather followed, and, with the proliferation of lady rodeo contestants and queens, some very ornate skirts evolved.

Collector interest in gear for ladies or youth seems only moderate, but exceptionally nice items are almost sure to appreciate.

251) Two old cotton riding skirts from the 'teens and a contemporary middy blouse from Sears, Roebuck and Co. These were worn by Goldie LeFevre of Meeker, Colorado.

252) This very elaborate, kid-leather riding skirt was made by Hamley and Co. of Pendleton and is the style worn by the Queen of the Pendleton Round Up in 1925. It originally cost forty-five pre-depression dollars.

SPURS

Perhaps no item of cowboy gear has elicited more attention, interest, and misunderstanding in recent years than spurs. The spurs currently most collectible are those made primarily between the two World Wars, when American spur-makers reached a zenith.

American cowboy spurs have evolved from two schools of tradition whose roots run separately all the way back to Spain. The earliest California, vaquero, or sometimes, *buckaroo* spurs retain the drop shanks and straight solid-buttoned heel bands of the conquistadors spurs. The most traditional ones will likely have chain slots, chap guards or *ganchitos* on part-round shanks, and an oval or square enlargement of the band at its juncture with the shank called the *rodete*. Despite some fanciful tall tales, the chap guard reflects a tradition and serves no real function.

The California spur-strap will likely be buckled inside the foot and often have a silver concho on the outside. The vaquero who wore them, removed his spurs when dismounted in the habit of his moccasined ancestors, and wore his spurs low with unequal double chains dangling.

To the east of the Rockies, the post-Civil War Texan and other plainsmen wore spurs from a variety of sources including California spurs, the patented Eurekas, O.K.'s, others from the East, and those big Mexican spurs which orginated in the area of Puebla, Mexico, but became largely known as *Chihuahuas*. These heavy Mexican spurs have wide, oval heel bands with swing buttons, large spoke rowels of 6 or 8 points, and, most frequently, a figure-eight motif in their shanks. The Texas cowboy wore Chihuahuas high on his booted heel, chainless, likely buckled on the outside, and took some pride, or so says the legend, in removing his spurs, pistol or hat virtually nowhere.

Though most early California spurs are unmarked, some will be marked by saddle-maker G.S. Garcia, Elko, Nevada, who from 1894 through 1932 employed numerous of the great and near-great California makers in his Elko shop. These include Estrada, Hernandez, Bernal, Herrera, Jayo, Gutierrez, and Morales. These makers moved on, carrying the California tradition east to Wyoming (Gutierrez) and north to Oregon (Morales).

Meanwhile, back at the ranch, McChesney, Kelly, Crockett, and other Anglo blacksmiths were beginning the Texas tradition of spur-making. Most of the more famous began in the Oklahoma-Texas border area around the turn-of-the-century. Though diverse, some Texas spurs show a definite heritage of the Chihuahua style, with swing buttons, heavy oval bands, and spoke rowels. Others have turned-up, button-heel bands with many pointed rowels. Many of these Texas spurs have the California-inspired chap guards, but most have somewhat straighter plain shanks. Long shanks without guards are sometimes called

Colorado or Rocky Mountain style. Concurrently, some very collectible figural shank styles evolved in lady-leg, gooseneck, eagle, or horse-head patterns. These were made prominently, if not originally, by John Robert McChesney. A basically Mexican style, the bottle opener shank was copied and popularized by Bianchi, and numerous other variations in shank styles blossomed.

Unlike both the California and Chihuahua spurs, in which the meticulous inlay of soft silver prevails, the Texas spurs tend to be mounted with overlays of hard silver alloys or other metals. The chief exceptions are Colorado prison-made spurs where the laborious, time-consuming inlay method predominates.

As the Texas makers and styles moved north and the Buckaroo tradition of California and Oregon came east, they met on the North Plains, especially in the area of Cheyenne, the Paris of cowboy fashion. Spurs from this area, as exemplified by Phillips-Gutierrez or Ed Hulbert, tend to combine the upturned bands or even swing buttons of the Texas spur with the stylish *ganchito*-adorned California shank. Some of these hybrids rank among the most beautiful of spurs, and their adornment often combines the overlay and inlay methods.

Finally competitive rodeo began to influence both styles. The preference of most bronc-riders of the 'teens and 1920s for heavy, long-shanked, large-roweled spurs whose very weight helped balance, gave way to lighter, eventually offset "Paddy Ryan" spurs that allowed freer leg action for impressing rodeo judges. Cutting horse men and ropers developed a taste for simpler elbow shanks, and traditional styles gave way to utility.

(SEE BITS, BOOTS)

253) Some of the earliest of Western spurs, these coarsely cast, moccasin spurs, were an Indian trade item in the fur era. The rowels are sharp and irregular, and they are slotted for thin, one-piece straps.

254) Buermann Star Brand Eureka #3 spurs were made of burnished sheet-metal. They had harness-style straps and were patented in the 1870s. They could be bought mail-order from Montgomery Ward for 30¢.

255) Buermann Star Brand #85 "OK" spurs were made of brushed steel and have 11/2" saw-blade rowels. Double-button OK spurs with their harness-style straps were an early cowboy favorite.

256) Another style of early patent spurs, these have sheet-metal heel-bands with painted card suits. These might be derisively called farmer or sheep-herder spurs.

257) These huge and elaborately decorated spurs originated in South America. They have extensive silver inlay.

258) Early Colonial or transitional Mexican spurs are scarcer than the Chihuahua style. This hard-worn pair has 3 1/4" ten-point rowels and dates from the mid-nineteenth century.

259) These chiseled iron Chihuahua spurs with huge 43/4" six-point rowels are typical of those worn by the early Texas trail drivers. Chihuahua spurs actually originate in the state of Puebla, Mexico.

260) This silver inlaid pair of Chihuahua spurs features 31/2" six-point rowels, and R.T. Frazier straps and was reportedly worn by the town marshal of Alamosa, Colorado, about 1915. Similar spurs of varying quality are still being made in Mexico.

261) A classical pair of early California vaquero spurs, these have engraved silver inlays on both sides, and silver bars on top edges and around shanks. They have 25/8" sharp, eight-point rowels, carved, buckskin-lined straps with silver conchos, and double heel chains.

262) Probably made in Sonora, Mexico, this unmarked pair of California style spurs features full silver inlays, bars, and 2" ten-point rowels. The *rodete*, or enlarged area of the heel bands' juncture with the shank, and the *ganchito,* hook, or chap guard, have traditional rather than functional purposes.

263) This worn pair of California spurs has engraved silver inlays on the outside only, silver concho straps, and a replaced rowel. The shaped California strap plate, *lamina del arco,* and chain slot, *raja para cadenillas,* can be seen in the rear.

264) *G.S. Garcia, Elko, Nev.* No. 5, coin-silver inlaid spurs sold in the 1914 catalog for $5.00. Uneven in quality but popular with collectors, Garcia spurs were made by a variety of spur and bit makers employed by the Elko saddle maker from 1896 to 1932.

265) With *Mike Morales, Maker, Portland* marked inside the band, these spurs have inlaid engraved silver on one side, around the shank, and in bars on top edges. They were acquired second-hand in 1925 by Idaho buckaroo Roy Olson. Morales was a premier Garcia maker who moved to Oregon.

266) Another pair of Morales, Portland spurs marked with his squashed *M* trademark under the buttons. These later California spurs have transitional features of turned-up heel-bands and 25/8" saw-blade rowels. They belonged to an Emmet, Idaho, buckaroo, the late Gene Timdell.

267) Though of probable California manufacture, these straighter-shanked spurs were usually cataloged as "Colorado Spurs." These have inlaid silver bars and 21/4" eight-point rowels and saw use on the Uintah-Ouray Reservation in eastern Utah.

268) Very large, heavy Cheyenne or Northern Plains spurs show a heritage of both California and Texas but evolved with early rodeo cowboys. These feature engraved inlaid silver bars and domed conchos on both sides and 2 3/4" thirty-two-point rowels. They were made by Rex Schnitker of Gillette, Wyoming.

269) These beautifully crafted silver and gold overlaid and inlaid spurs are marked *E.H.* for Wyoming maker, Ed Hulbert. They combine the swing button Texas bands with a stylish California shank.

270) These fancy sterling silver and gold-mounted spurs were made by Edward Bohlin of Hollywood for Bern Gregory in the 1930s. The sterling conchos and buckles are also marked Bohlin.

271) August Buermann Star Brand spurs #1476 feature silver bar inlays on both sides and 21/8" ten-point rowels. Buermann was easily the largest of bit and spur makers and manufactured, as his catalog claimed, "from the cheapest to the very best."

272) August Buermann's #1471 "Roosevelt" spurs are the very top of the Star Brand line. A classic California style, they feature extensive engraved silver inlays, double chains, and 13/4" ten-point rowels.

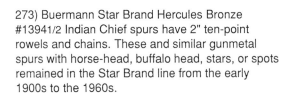

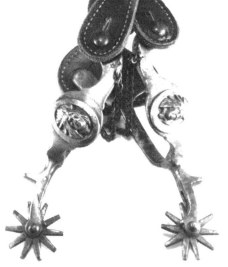

273) Buermann Star Brand Hercules Bronze #13941/2 Indian Chief spurs have 2" ten-point rowels and chains. These and similar gunmetal spurs with horse-head, buffalo head, stars, or spots remained in the Star Brand line from the early 1900s to the 1960s.

274) Lady-leg spurs by their probable inventor, J.R. McChesney. His spurs are usually unmarked but recognizable. The legs have rounded contours.

275) Classic spurs by the father of Texas-Oklahoma spur makers, John Robert McChesney, this twist-shank style was cataloged by Shipley as "No. 1 Spur, Style L, full mounted, per pair — $3.75." They have the arm-and-hammer trade-mark.

276) Later McChesney spurs were manufactured by Nocona Boot Co. with the name in large letters inside the heel band. These feature engraved silver overlays on one side of the upturned bands, solid buttons, and 2" twelve-point rowels. Even later, the name appears in small letters under the button.

277) These large, classic Texas *Kelly Bros.* spurs with engraved silver alloy overlays, swing buttons, and big 3" six-point rowels distinctly reflect their Chihuahua heritage. P.M. Kelly is another giant of the Texas spur tradition.

278) *C.P. Shipley, Kan City, Mo.* marked inside the band of No. 8 Leg Pattern spurs. Enoch Phelps, a 1920s Trinidad, Colorado, cowboy, wore these silver and copper-mounted "gal-legs" many miles. Note the severe wear at rowel center. One pin is worn through.

279) Two more pairs of *Kelly Bros.* spurs, the Montana Joe style on the left and *X*-marked, gooseneck style on the right. The Kellys used both X's and O's on second-line spurs.

280) These *K.B. & P.* stamped spurs have an overlaid silver scroll, one-piece dove-wing straps, and replaced notched rowels. The P is for Clyde Parker, who had worked, along with P.M. Kelly, for John Robert\ McChesney.

281) *Powder River* was the brand name of the famous Denver Dry Goods Co. These two pairs were worn by West Slope Colorado cowboys of the 1930s.

282) These unusual spurs were made from strips of stainless-steel silver soldered together by Bill Lamphere of Bountiful, Utah, about 1940. They were used by the author's father, the late Al Mackin.

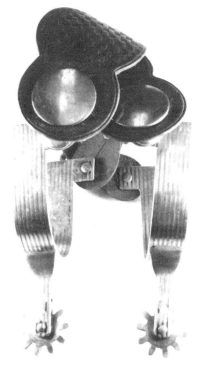

283) Canon City, Colorado, prison-made spurs featuring bird-head shanks, double engraved inlaid mountings, well-domed, solid buttons on upturned bands, and 2", hand-filed rowels. Others may have a prisoner number.

284) *By F.B.* marks the work of later Canon City maker Frank Bradney. These spurs are of the "Paddy Ryan" bronc-spur style, which became popular in the 1930s. They are overlaid with silver and gold.

285) "Ricardo" was a Denver silversmith and quality spur maker who came to prominence in the 1940s. These nickel silver spurs have full engraved sterling silver overlay covering band, shank, and 21/8", sixteen-point rowels.

286) Like most bits and spurs marked *Garcia*, these post-war, silver-overlayed trophy spurs were imported from Amozoc, Mexico, near Puebla.

287) Early, heavy, rodeo bronc-rider spurs made by Charles Wyatt, Maybell, Colorado, for Chuck Roberts in 1926. They have a quarter-circle over circle maker mark. The holes in the shanks are for tie-down thongs, and their heavy weight helped balance.

288) The late Frank Longtine of Riverton, Wyoming, made this pair of unmarked concho and arrow design spurs the winter of 1932 while a cowboy on the Big Sandy. Most *shop* or unmarked spurs are difficult to identify.

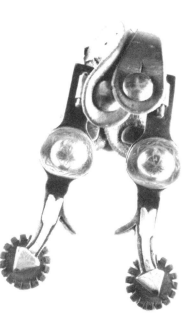

289) Left, unmarked Buermann #12801/2 malleable iron spurs with the fancy, 8-point rowels sometimes called "snow flakes" by collectors. Early nickel-plated cast-iron spurs with chains. The crescent and cross design has remnants of red enamel.

290) Colonial-style youth spurs with danglers, or "jingle-bobs" in cowboy lore. They are found infrequently and usually on cheap spurs.

291) Left: These drop-shank, California-style spurs are marked with North and Judd's anchor near the buttons. The late cast spurs to the right have an anchor on top of the shank.

292)) This nice old pair of Bullhead Crock-etts are marked inside the band and were won at a Browning, Montana rodeo by contemporary Old West character Pax Baker, past sheriff of Lake County, Colo-rado.

293) Crockett "Colorado Special" spurs have engraved silver on out-side buttons only. Long, plain shank spurs are often cataloged as Colo-rado or Rocky Mountain style. These were the author's "users."

294) These 1930s Crockett ro-deo bronc spurs have shanks reminiscent of Chihuahua spurs. Light, swing-button, star-roweled spurs permitted more leg action than their heavy predecessors. A tie-down thong would have been wrapped around the shank and the boot heel.

295) Early Crockett spurs were burnished like these "Denver Specials" to the left or blued. Progression of marks is O. Crockett inside band, Crockett inside band, small letters below button, larger letters below button, on edge near juncture of shank and band, and finally on edge below the buttons.

296) From left, the nickeled edge marked *Crockett* "arrow shank" spurs of Henry Schaefermeyer of Vernal, Utah. Crockett "Cherokee" or bottle-opener shank spurs, and later Crockett-Renalde dress spurs marked with a C and R within a horseshoe.

297) Crocketts all, from left, stainless spurs with bronze eagles; nickeled cowboy spurs with chap guards; and a pair of bronc spurs with unusual tie-down loops and clover rowels.

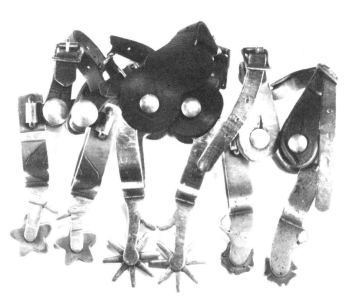

298) Late spurs for specialist cowboys, the Kelly bullrider spurs #215 have 2" shank with 15-degree offset, and these silver-mounted Crocketts have the elbow shank favored by rodeo ropers and cutting-horse men.

299) Modern Mexican spurs of nice quality are often marketed by American firms. The pair to the left are blued and sterling inlaid and have engraved domed buttons. To the right, a gooseneck design with engraved silver alloy overlays.

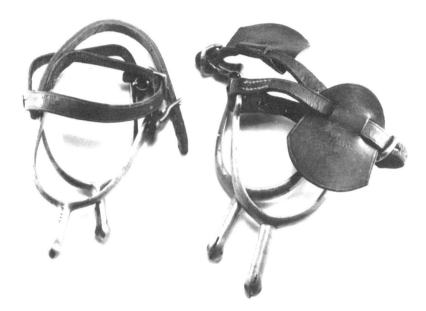

300) Military spurs, like bits, find some favor with Western collectors. Left, the last and most common U.S. Cavalry spurs, roweless steel alloy. To the right, Canadian Cavalry and NWMP spurs with Broad Arrow proof and marked *Ottawa, 1911*, on their strap.

301) U.S. Cavalry spurs made of brass and marked *R.I.A., 1906*. These are the last of the cavalry spurs with rowels.

302) Another pair of small-roweled, elbow-shanked cutting horse or roping spurs, these were marked *E.F. Blanchard Yucca-Ariz. No. 5 PS*. This prominent Arizona and New Mexico maker died recently.

303) Gal-leg spurs marked *Hall* are by contemporary maker Carl Hall of Commanche, Texas. Increased interest and values of old spurs have led many modern makers to emulate the old-timers.

304) Contour fitted spurs, such as this nice quality but unmarked bronze pair, and spurs made of aluminum and stainless steel get little attention from collectors.

305) Pot-metal-cast toy spurs have been available and popular with cowtots at least since the 1920s. Primarily toys, they lack the durability, weight, and quality of youth spurs.

306) Red Bunn of Rifle, Colorado, helped his uncle, Sam Bunn, make these huge novelty spurs at his ranch forge on Divide Creek in the early 1930s, "just for fun." They have 5" nine-point rowels on five-inch shanks. He made the smaller goose-necks from rake teeth in the 1940s.

307) Another novelty, these wooden spurs were whittled by some unknown cowboy and found in an old home by Nancy Hockemeyer at Maybell, Colorado.

STICKING TOMMY

Actually not a cowboy item at all, the sticking Tommy, or miner's candlestick holder, may well turn up in barns or old timers' gear. Most are machine manufactured, but the hand-forged ones and especially the fancy or folding ones are very desirable collector's items.

308) An unusually ornate sticking Tommy with piercings and brass adornment. This was a labor of love by some old skilled blacksmith.

STINGY GUNS

As any Western-movie fan knows, not all Old West guns were the big six-shooters and saddle rifles. There were also those diminutive little pistols that were slipped inconspicuously in gambler's cuff, cowboy's boot, and somewhat alluringly down the dance hall gal's bodice.

These tiny pistols were the cartridge-era out-growth of Henry Deringer's little percussion pistol. Some, like the Colt Thuer and Remington Double Deringer, were, like their namesake predecessors, large, .41 caliber pistols. Others, like the Colt Open Top and New-Line seven-shooters, fired the puny .22 rimfire cartridge. All provided chap pocket-size protection at poker-table ranges.

Collectors interest in these little guns is usually centered in the true deringer models or the popular names, Colt, Remington, and Smith and Wesson. Increasing interest is also developing in other "suicide special" or bureau-drawer revolvers, especially those with spur triggers.

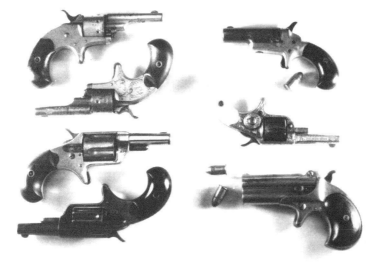

309) Typical hide-out pistols of the Wild West are these Colt Open Top . 22 Caliber, seven-shot revolvers; Colt NewLine .32 Caliber Revolvers; Colt Third Model Thuer Deringer; NewLine .22 Revolver; and the Remington Double Deringer.

STIRRUPS

Because stirrups have a fascinating and relatively recent history, during which they played a great role in world conquest and medieval knighthood, all the cowboy had to do was refine them. Their usefulness and importance had been thoroughly established by his predecessors.

In California, vaqueros began to spurn the large, drilled-block Mexican or Santa Fe stirrups and adopted the lighter, Anglo, bentwood styles, the "dog house" stirrups of the plainsmen. These were ultimately modified into the "Visalia" stirrups. As stiff-countered cowboy boots became universal, cowboys experimented with narrower, ox-bow styles that were easy to grasp.

In the 1890s, several patented metal stirrups evolved, and brass or iron-ring stirrups were popular in the 'teens, even in the cold, northern country where they helped frost-bite numbed feet. Any cowboy who ever caught an iron stirrup behind the ear while reaching under for the belly-band quickly dumped them!

Stirrup collectors—and such do exist, even for singles—are usually more interested in the patent, break-a-way, side saddle, or very old and exotic items. Another group of collectors are on the lookout for good, serviceable pairs to restore old stock saddles. Early bent-wood and attractive ox-bows are desirable.

310) These Turner patent, ventilated-iron stirrups were one of several styles and patents developed in the 1890s. Metal stirrups lost favor because they were cold.

311) Iron-ring stirrups were popular from the turn-of-the-century until the 1920s, especially in the Rocky Mountains. They were easier to grasp with a booted foot than flat-treaded Visalias, especially on rambunctious horses.

312) These fancy, silver-inlaid brass stirrups originated in Mexico for the charros, but *gringo* cowboys also liked the flash.

TAPADEROS

Literally from the Spanish "things that cover," *tapaderos* are covers for the stirrup and foot. On the earliest vaquero's saddle, they were a round, leather shield at the front of the drilled-oak stirrup used to protect his sandal-exposed toes.

Another style was simply a shield of leather curved around the stirrup-front and fastened top and bottom. These were common to many old stock saddles and the early McClellan Cavalry saddles. They seem to be popular, too, on modern pony saddles.

Finally, there are the fully closed and sometimes wool-fleece-lined taps designed to give substantial protection to the rider. The abbreviated short, snubby ones are usually called bull-dogs, and those with long wings are "monkey-nosed" or "eagle-billed."

As with stirrups, taps have become somewhat collectible in their own right, but they are especially valuable in pairs to restore old saddles. Famous-maker names and fancy tooling give greatest values.

313) These are the simpler, shield-style tapaderos used on both stock and military saddles. The leather front helps protect the boot and keep it from sliding through the stirrup.

314) Fully, enclosed, bull-dog taps offer greater protection. They are often lined with wool fleece to keep the rider's feet warm and dry. This pair was made by "Powder River," a trade name of the Denver Dry Goods Co.

315) Long, flowing tapaderos may be extensively tooled and sometimes silver-mounted. They are characteristic of later California saddles and may run as long as 28".

WATCH FOBS

One post-1900 item that has received considerable collector interest in the last few years is the Western watch fob, especially those marketed by the old saddle makers. Hamley and Co., for example, sold a watch fob representation of its 1914 Pendleton Round-Up trophy saddle for 24¢ in the 'teens and for 30¢ in 1935.

Demand had driven the price of these fobs to hundreds of times their original costs in the early 1980s, and, predictably, almost undetectable reproductions have now become available. It seems inescapable that when items that cost only a few cents to begin with become grossly inflated, someone will make them again.

Collector demand remains for old watch fobs, dampened to some extent by the numerous fakes available.

316) A variety of Western-styled watch fob ornaments including a tiny brass stirrup. None have particular advertising significance and are, therefore, less collectible.

317) Very collectible watch fobs include a holstered pistol, a "Wyoming Ranchman Outfitters" saddle, and saddle fobs by Frazier, Pueblo and Hamley, Pendleton. The last two have been extensively copied.

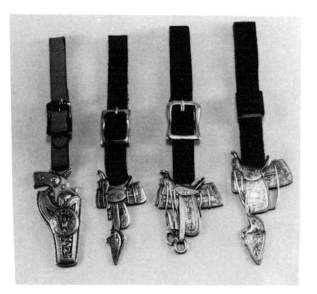

WINCHESTERS

While Winchester's claim of being the "Gun that won the West" is highly debatable, its nearly universal appeal to cowboys is beyond question. Though the major owner of the predecessor, New Haven Arms Co., industrial magnate Oliver F. Winchester introduced his own namesake in 1866, an improved-loading-system Henry lever-action repeater. Puny in power when compared to the big single-shot rifles then in vogue with Western hunters, the lighter brass-framed "Yellow Boy" rifle had a magazine capacity of seventeen rimfire cartridges, lots of firepower for the mounted fighter.

This toggle-link design was further improved by the iron framed Model 1873 in that year and the larger hunting cartridge repeater, the Model 1876. Winchester, who had developed the famous center fire 44-40 cartridge and bought out several competitors, was simply without peer in the West. Then, about 1878, Colt began to chamber its popular single-action frontier revolver for the same Winchester .44 center-fire, and the horseman could load either arm with the same cartridges. Similar chamberings were offered for the .32 W.C.F(32-20) and .38 W.C.F(38-40) in the 1880s. Thus was born this most popular cowboy duo.

Also in the 1880s, the Winchester firm, under son-in-law T.G. Bennett, acquired the first of numerous gun designs from Ogden, Utah, genius John M. Browning. These patents were to keep Winchester well in the lead of competition through the turn-of-the-century and would include the famous Model 1894, which is still made and chambered in thirty-thirty.

Two schools of thought seem evident in Winchester collectors. To one school, near-new condition is the primary requisite for value, and astounding prices have been paid recently for old guns in unused condition. In the West, where Winchesters were often used hard, more interest seems to be paid to the appeal and rarity of the almost endless variations that were made. Originality is important in either case, and old Winchesters should <u>never</u> be altered or refinished without expert advice.

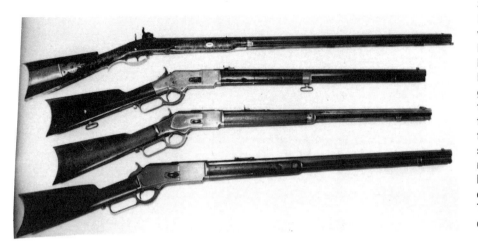

318) From the top: The original Kentucky long rifle evolved in many ways. This New England half stock, like the Plains rifle, was a shorter, horseman's gun. The Model 1866 has a wooden forearm and brass or gun-metal receiver and was the first to bear the Winchester name. The famous Model 1873 was Winchester's first center-fire and probably the standard cowboy rifle. The Centennial Model 1876 was the last and the largest of the toggle-link action Winchesters. Popular with hunters like Teddy Roosevelt, it sold less than one-tenth as well as the 1873.

319) From the top: First of the Browning patents to be manufactured by Winchester, the Model 1885 Single Shot rifle was made in the greatest number of calibers and variations of all Winchester rifles. The Model 1886, like the 1876 it supplanted, was a large-caliber hunter's rifle. It had several chamberings, including the .45.70.405, the then-standard military cartridge. This one is also stamped *Browning Bros. Ogden, U.T.* Also popular with Teddy Roosevelt, the Model 1895 Winchester has a box magazine beneath the frame, which gives it a distinctive look among Winchesters.

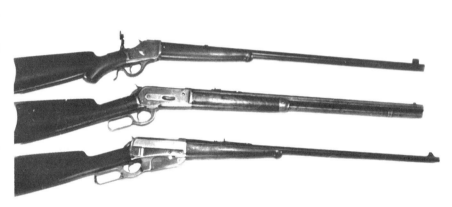

320) John Browning also introduced pump or trombone actions to the Winchester line. The rifles top and bottom are octagon-barreled Model 1890s in the .22 short and .22 W.R.F. respectively. The center rifle is a Model 1906, which will shoot .22 short, long, or long rifle. These were standard small-game-getters around many Western bunkhouses.

321) Perhaps the most beautiful of the Winchesters, the Model 1892 is a movie standard. John Wayne and the Rifleman used them, and more than a few have even mysteriously appeared in Civil War epics! Pictured are standard round and octagon-barreled rifles, and a scarce deluxe take-down rifle with checkered pistol-grip and extra-grade wood. Wood stocks on Winchesters are sometimes graded by X's inside the tang inletting.

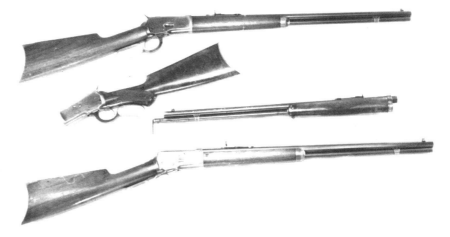

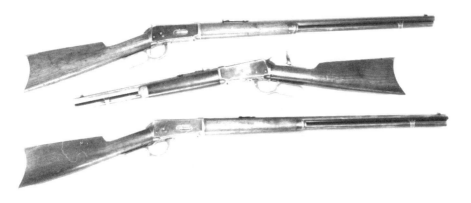

322) The most popular of all sporting rifles, over four million Model 1894 and '94 Winchesters have been made. The top and bottom guns are early ones in .32-40 and .38-55 with round and octagon barrels. All things being equal, octagon barrels are premium on most Winchester models. Center is a very rare Winchester variation, a factory original, 16", octagon-barreled, short rifle. Note that the forearm is also shorter than standard. Most shorter-than-standard rifles were modified after leaving the factory, and some are outright fakes.

323) The first and last of the old Cowboy carbines, this 1866 .44 caliber is marked by the Republic of Mexico. The excellent condition model 1895 in .30 U.S. once belonged to an El Paso pharmacist with a penchant for raids into Mexico.

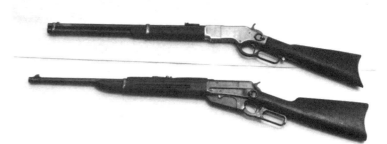

324) The great cowboy duo, Winchester and Colt, in similar caliber. Saddle-ring carbines, such as this Model 1873 in .32 W.C.F. caliber, scarce in the 1873 carbine, are popular with collectors. Carbines can be found in most models and can usually be distinguished by shorter barrels, the ring around the forearm, a less-pronounced curved butt-plate, and, until about 1926, the saddle ring on the left of the receiver.

325) Shotguns, too, saw use against both man and game on the Western frontier. The 1893 pump (top) is serial #200. The lever-action 1887 model below is a ten-gauge. Like most pre-1900 Winchesters, they are John Browning patents.

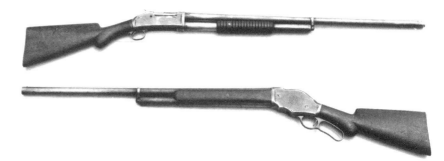

326) Two popular hunting rifles of the 1880s, the Model 1885 single shot in .32-40 at top, and a special-ordered, Freund-sighted model 1886 in .45-90 with several rare features, below. Two Mills civilian cartridge belts are in the center.

327) A truly rare Winchester, this only known Highwall short rifle was manufactured with an original 15", number 3, .25-35 caliber barrel. It won the NRA distinguished weapon medal in 1978 and has been exempted from federal regulations. Original configuration of most early Winchesters can be documented by contacting the Winchester Museum at the Buffalo Bill Historical Center, Box 100, Cody, Wyoming 82414.

PRICE GUIDE

COVER

Meanea, left hand, tooled, 7½", S. A. Holster	$3200 to $3800
Unmarked money/cartridge belt, 32-20 loops	$250 to $350
Rio Blanco Sheriff's Posse badge	$150 to $225
Colt Frontier, 7½", made 1881, steer head ivory grips	$2500 to $4500

COLOR PLATE, page vi

Frazier studded chaps, "WILD HORSE JACK", sterling	$8000 to $9500
Cox made, Canon City prison spurs	$3200 to $3800
Heiser cantana pommel bag holster	$1500 to $1800
Colt 7½" Peacemaker, ivory grips	$1800 to $2200
Bregenzer saddle	$1200 to $1600

ADVERTISING, page 3

Photo #1	Colt Tex and Patches poster, (several variations)	$750 to $1100
#2	Buffalo Bill statue	$75 to $125
#2	101 Ranch Poster	$300 to $400
#3	Jo Mora, sweethearts poster, (variations, reprints)	$300 to $400
#4	Salt Lake County or Moffat County (each)	$75 to $125
#5	C.B.&Q. Railroad Police	$110 to $125
#5	Stock City Marshal	$200 to $300
#5	Rio Blanco County Sheriff's Posse	$150 to $225
#5	Salt Lake County Sheriff's Posse	$100 to $175
#6	Police Chief, Bingham Canyon, Utah, hallmarked, breast	$150 to $200
#6	Police Chief, Bingham Canyon, Utah, hat badge	$50 to $75
#6	Utah State Prison Guard, hallmarked	$50 to $100
#6	Corrections Officer, Wyoming State Prison	$50 to $100
#7	Salt Lake City, Special Police #1464	$50 to $100
#7	Salt Lake City, Special Police #476	$40 to $80
#7	Express Company	$75 to $125
#7	Stock City Marshal	$175 to $225
#8	Constable, Bunkerville (Nev.), with name	$75 to $100
#8	Utah Indian War medal, ribbon	$250 to $350
#8	Town Marshal (reproduction)	$30 to $50
#8	Deputy U.S. Marshal (doubtful authenticity)	$40 to $75

BELTS, page 8

#9	Model 1876 U.S. Prairie Belt	$325 to $400
#9	Model 1880 U.S. Mills belt, cast two piece buckle	$500 to $550
#9	Civilian Mills wider rifle cartridge belt, dog-head plate	$100 to $150
#9	Civilian Mills narrower pistol cartridge belt, dog-head plate	$100 to $150
#9	Winchester wider rifle cartridge belt, bear-head plate	$500 to $600
#9	Winchester 44-40 cartridge belt, bear-head plate	$600 to $700

BELTS, continued, pages 8 to 10

Photo #10	38 caliber cartridge belt	$35 to $75
#10	32-20 cartridge belt, seperate tongue, billet	$75 to $150
#10	Brigham Patent marked belt	$100 to $125
#10	Lawrence marked, 45 caliber cartridge belt	$75 to $150

#10	Money/cartridge combination belt	$200 to $300
#10	Large combined rifle, pistol cartridge belt	$75 to $100
#11	Leather shotgun shell belts (each)	$40 to $75
#12	Ranch made, Texas star spotted bronc belt	$50 to $100
#12	Unmarked bronc belt	$25 to $50
#12	Keyston made and marked bronc belt	$50 to $75
#13	Hand fashioned bronc belt with swastika	$275 to $325
#14	Gallup extensively studded bronc belt	$400 to $500
#14	Lawrence studded bronc belt	$250 to $300
#15	Older Ute beaded squaw belt	$650 to $800

BITS, pages 13 to 23

#16	Early, unmarked Santa Barbara spade	$550 to $750
#17	California, fish motif spade	$375 to $475
#18	Commercial, silver inlaid, loose jaw spade	$250 to $350
#19	Commercial, nickel mounted, solid-jaw spade	$75 to $125
#20	Messing bird-head, half breed	$400 to $500
#21	Buermann "Arizona" spade	$450 to $600
#22	Bird-head, half-breed	$30 to $50
#23	Buermann #406 silver inlaid half-breed	$225 to $300
#24	Buermann "Star" silver inlaid half-breed	$500 to $800
#25	Buermann #1373 buffalo-head half-breed	$450 to $500
#26	Morales #36 silver inlaid half-breed	$750 to $900
#27	Concho and crescent style (altered, hurts price a lot)	$350 to $500
#28	Unmarked Las Cruces (altered, hurts price a little)	$300 to $350
#29	Arsenal marked and dated U.S. Model 1859	$225 to $275
#30	U.S. Model 1874 Shoemaker	$175 to $225
#31	Buermann Shoemaker copy	$125 to $175
#32	U.S. Model 1909 cavalry	$25 to $35
#33	Buermann bronze Panama style	$60 to $80
#34	Crockett silver mounted hearts and bars	$75 to $100
#35	Left: Kelly Bros. gal-leg, mounted	$225 to $275
#35	Right: McChesney gal-leg, mounted (unmarked)	$225 to $275
#36	Shop made, heart mounted, Texas curb	$35 to $50
#37	Hall contemporary gal-leg, mounted	$100 to $125
#38	Left: cast metal gal-leg	$60 to $80
#38	Star Steel gal-leg	$125 to $150
#39	Shop made aluminum nude	$75 to $125
#40	Rearing horse style	$125 to $175
#41	Mexican ring bit	$20 to $35
#42	Silver inlaid Mexican curb bit	$50 to $100
#43	Early, intricate Mexican bit	$75 to $100
#44	Modern Mexican gal-leg	$40 to $65
#45	Commercial mule ring bit	$100 to $135
#46	Anchor Brand S-shank roping bit	$35 to $45
#47	Late Crockett silver overlay on blue steel	$75 to $100
#48	Late Garcia silver overlay on stainless	$125 to $150
#49	San Angelo Easy Stop patented hackamore bit	$25 to $35

BLANKETS, pages 25 and 26

Photo #50	Tans and brown double saddle blanket	$200 to $500
#51	Red, black, and greys double saddle blanket	$200 to $500
#52	Grey, white, and red double saddle blanket	$200 to $500
#53	3' by 5' well woven rug	$250 to $600
#54	4' by 5' intricate pattern rug	$1100 to $1700

BOOKS, pages 28 and 29

#55	*My Life on the Range*, Clay	$200 to $300
#55	*Thirty One Years on the Plains*, Drannan	$25 to $40

#55	*Ten Years a Cowboy*, Post	$25 to $40
#56	*Buffalo Bill*, autographed by him	$450 to $550
#57	*Nevada Brand Book*, 1946	$60 to $80
#57	*Colorado Brand Book*, 1948	$50 to $60
#58	*Wyoming Brand Books*, 1912 to 1956, (early to late, each)	$200 to $250
#59, 60	*Stock Yards* cowboy tally book	$50 to $85

BOOTS, pages 32 to 35

#61	Early stove pipe, 1880s	$1200 to $1500
#61	Silver and copper inlaid spurs	$250 to $350
#62	Black with stove pipe tops, 1890s	$1000 to $1250
#62	Indianola, leather covered bands, studded straps	$75 to $125
#63	Lower vee cut, white leather inlays, 1900s	$100 to $150
#63	Ricardo plain nickel-silver steel	$75 to $100
#64	Wing tip and extensive stitching	$75 to $125
#64	Buermann double gal-leg style spurs	$175 to $250
#65	Kirkendall with cactus inlays	$150 to $200
#65	Shop made spurs with concho straps	$125 to $200
#66	Multi-colored Mexican boots with inlays, exotic leather	$175 to $250
#66	Contoured heel silver overlaid spurs, small	$75 to $110
#67	Lady's laced high boots	$50 to $110
#67	Shop made by George LeFevre, Rocky Mountain style	$75 to $110

BRANDING IRONS, page 37

#68	Early ox yoke stamp iron	$50 to $75
#68	Hand wrought running iron	$75 to $110
#68	Commercial steel and brass iron	$35 to $50
#69, 70, 71	Various hand wrought stamp branding irons	$25 to $75

BRIDLES, pages 39 to 42

#72	Wyoming Prison, Rawlins, round and flat horsehair hitched	$2700 to $3200
#73	Wyoming Prison, flat horsehair hitch work in leather	$1000 to $1350
#74	Canon City, horsehair and synthetic, colorful	$1000 to $1200
#75	Canon City prison, black and white, used, some damage	$300 to $400
#76	Wyoming, braided leather and horsehair headstall	$700 to $750
#77	Walla Walla prison, used and faded horsehair	$350 to $500
#78	Braided leather head with glass buffalo rosettes	$150 to $300
#79	Boise prison bridle head, dyed horsehair, damaged	$150 to $250
#80	Kansas City Stock Yards Co. marked work bridle	$75 to $125
#81	Large and ornately mounted plains style	$600 to $900
#82	Silver mounted California head stall	$100 to $150
#83	Red and black wool adorned Mexican bridle	$25 to $60
#84	Navajo silver and turquois adorned bridle	$400 to $500

CARTRIDGES, page 44

Photo #85	(All full, original cartridges and boxes) top, left, 1876	$75 to $100
#85	Top, right, 1886	$100 to $125
#85	Left, middle, 1895	$30 to $50
#85	Right, middle and left bottom, 1894	$30 t0 $40
#85	Right, bottom, bear on box, 1895	$25 to $35
#86	32-20 boxed ammo, items to left	$30 to $50
#86	32-20, semi-modern (clean, full boxes), to the right	$25 to $35
#87	Various old 1894 caliber boxed ammo, all full	$45 to $75

CATALOGS, pages 46 to 51

#88	Donnel saddle shop photo studio card	$100 to $165
#89	R.T. Frazier 1927 saddle catalog, all types of tack	$200 t0 $300
#89	Victor Marden 1910 saddle catalog	$100 to $150
#89	Blake Miller, Cheyenne, Catalog #12	$150 to $250
#90	Pawnee Bill's Indian Trading Post, Pawnee, Oklahoma	$100 to $150

#90	Strong Curio Co., South Dakota Indian traders	$75 to $150
#91	R.J. Andrew, Concho Brand Saddles, 1914	$75 to $150
#91	Hamley's Cowboy Catalog, 1925-1926	$150 to $250
#91	Visalia Stock Saddle Co., #22	$125 to $175
#92	Visalia Stock Saddle Co. #31	$150 to $200
#92	Hamley's Cowboy Catalog #35	$75 to $90
#92	N. Porter Saddle and Harness, 1935	$100 to $125
#92	Read Brothers, Ogden, 1930s	$75 to $100
#93	Hamley catalogs, 1915 (#10) to 1941 (#41), oldest to newest	$300 to $60
#94	N. Porter catalogs #22,23,25,26 (all in 1930s) each	$100 to $175
#95	Western Saddle Mfg. Co., 1930s	$35 to $40
#95	H.H. Heiser, holsters and gun leather	$30 to $45
#95	H.H. Heiser, saddles and tack	$45 to $65
#96	Denver Dry Goods, "Powder River", 1935	$35 to $50
#96	White and Davis, Pueblo	$35 to $50
#96	Stockman Farmer, Denver, 1934-1935, Stetson cover	$25 to $30
#96	Fred Mueller, Denver, #76	$25 to $35
#97	Variety of 1930s mail order catalogs for stockmen, (each)	$25 to $35
#98	Visalia catalog #33, late 1930s	$100 to $150
#98	Garcia Saddlery, Salinas, late 1930s	$75 to $85
#98	N. Porter, #34, late 1930s	$50 ,to $75
#98	Shipley's Saddlerygram, flyer and brief catalog	$15 to $25
#98	Bohlin, Hollywood, 1940 (soiled condition)	$75 to $125
#99	Stern's, San Jose, 1938	$100 to $125
#99	Visalia catalog #32, 1930s	$100 to $150
#99	Newell's Saddle Shop, Western Stock Saddles, St. Louis	$45 to $60
#99	Lawrence, Sporting Goods (gun leather) and Saddles	$15 to $20
#100	Big 1950s catalogs (each)	$30 to $75
#101	Heiser saddle catalogs (early to late)	$125 to $50
#101	Heiser gun leather catalogs (early to late)	$125 to $30
#102	S,D, Myres seperate saddle and gun leather catalogs	$30 to $100
#103	Thomson & Son sporting goods, 1878	$15 to $20
#104	Browning Bros., Ogden (all, each)	$50 to $70

CATALOGS, continued, pages 51 and 52

Photo #105	Sporting goods mail order catalogs from the teens	$15 to $30
#106, 107	Nocona Boots	$25 to $30
#106, 107	David Posada Boots, Hollywood	$25 to $35
#106, 107	Everson-Ross Badges, 1910	$60 to $80
#108	North and Judd, Anchor Brand	$25 to $30
#108	Morales #3 Price List and catalog supplement	$100 to $150
#109	Reproduced catalogs printed in the 1980s	$10 to $25

CHAPS, pages 54 to 57

#110	Marden, fringed shotgun	$500 t0 $750
#111	Mexican leather vaquero pants	$300 to $500
#112	Heiser fringed shotguns with conchos	$650 to $850
#113	Gallup floral tooled, fringed, conchos (near new cond)	$2200 to $2800
#114	Meanea black angoras, tooled belt (near new cond)	$3800 to $4800
#115	Heiser youth's gold angoras (near new cond)	$1500 to $1800
#116	Miles City red-brown angoras	$900 to $1100
#117	Snyder white angoras	$700 to $800
#118	Lawrence "pinto", black and white angoras	$1100 to $1500
#119	Ranch made buffalo skin chaps	$400 to $600
#120	Furstnow special order extra wide batwings	$300 to $500
#121	Hamley studded and rearing horse conchos, hearts	$2000 to $2500

COATS, page 59

#122	Gordon and Ferguson fine quality hair-on horsehide	$500 to $750

#123	Wyoming made winter killed horse (often called bear!)	$300 to $400
#124	Broadside for Douglas, Wyoming fur and hide dealer	$25 to $30
#124	Catalog for Globe Tanning, coat and robe makers	$20 to $25
#125	Ordinary quality horsehide coat	$200 to $300

COLTS, pages 62 to 64

Please, remember that very slight variations in firearms can make drastic differences in their prices.

#126	First Model Dragoon, Fluck type, 1848, very good condition	$7500 to $9000
#126	1849 Pocket, small guard, very good condition	$700 to $800
#126	1849 Pocket Model, fine condition	$700 to $850
#127	1851 Navy, fine condition	$1000 to $1400
#127	1851 Navy, very good condition	$700 to $800
#127	1851 Navy, excellent except front sight altered	$1200 to $1600
#128	1860 Army Model, fine	$1500 to $1700
#128	1862 Pocket of Navy Caliber, very good	$500 to $650
#128	1862 Police Model, excellent	$700 to $850
#129	Richards conversion of 1860 Army, fine	$1600 to $1800
#129	3½" conversion of Pocket Model, 38 R.F.	$700 to $850
#130	Civilian 7½" Peacemaker, 1881, excellent	$2000 to $2500
#130	Cavalry Model, #5126, Custer massacre survivor	$5000 to $20,000
#130	Artillery Model, near match, fine	$1000 to $1600
#131	Black powder .38 Colt 7½" nickeled S.A., very good	$1200 to $1600
#131	Ivory gripped Peacemaker, (same as color plate)	$1800 to $2200
#132	Etched Frontier, carved ivory, excellent (same as cover)	$4000 to $4500
#132	Stamped Frontier, eagle grips, fine (broken trigger tip)	$1200 to $1400
#132	Blue and case Frontier, eagle grips, fine	$1500 to $2000
#132	Smokeless powder Frontier, excellent	$1200 to $1400
#133	Bisleys, preference to longer barrel and larger calibers	$800 to $1400
#134	Smokeless S.A.s, 45 or 41 bring most, fine to excel.	$1200 to $1750

COLTS, continued, pages 65 and 66

Photo #135	Smokeless 44-40 S.A., excellent plus	$1700 to $1900
#135	Nickeled, smokeless 32-20, fine except later stag grips	$750 to $900
#135	Long flute variation, 45 Colt, fine	$2000 to $2400
#136	Blue and cased 38 Colt Lightning, excellent	$400 to $550
#136	Etched 41 D.A. "Thunderer", no ejector, excellent	$450 to $550
#137	Nickeled 45 Colt 7½" 1878 D.A., fine	$500 to $800
#137	Blued 44-40, 7½", 1878 D.A., fine	$500 to $800
#137	Blued 45 Colt 6" 1878-1902 Phillipine, excellent	$850 to $950
#138	Model 1889 swing out cylinder, 4½" 38 Colt, fine	$300 to $400
#138	Model 1889, 41 Colt, 6", near new condition	$400 to $600
#139	Engraved, steer-head pearl, 41 Colt Army Special, excellent	$4000 to $5000
#139	Blued 32-20 Army Special, 6", 32-20, excellent	$400 to $600
#140	Colt Burgess "Baby" carbine, ultra light, very good	$2800 to $3200
#140	Lightning slide action 38-40 octagon rifle, excellent	$700 to $900
#140	Lightning 22 caliber octagon rifle, fine	$450 to $550
#141	New Service 7½" 45 Colt, excellent	$400 to $550
#141	Pearl gripped New Police, excellent!	$150 to $300
#141	Rubber gripped, nickel New Police, excellent	$100 to $200
#142	Boxed Pocket Positive, excellent	$250 to $350

CUFFS, pages 68 to 70

#143	Frazier, ribbon tooled, new condition	$250 to $400
#144	Heiser, ribbon tooled	$150 to $250
#145	Bregenzer, hand tooled ribbon edge, show use	$200 to $300
#146	Snyder Saddles, floral leaf tooling	$100 to $150
#147	Gopher Brand longhorn steer motif	$150 to $225
#148	Hand tooled Indian head, substantial use	$150 to $200
#149	Scalloped 8", studs, conchos, basket weave,	$250 to $350

#150	Floral tooled, studs, Texas star, light russt color	$250 to $350
#151	Probably Porter, three swastika snaps, ribbon tooled	$175 to $225
#152	Smaller Indian head and floral, buckle closures	$100 to $1500
#153	Lady or youth's simple geometric tooling	$50 to $100
#154	T. Flynn, nickel spots, Texas star, conchos	$400 to $500

GAUNTLETS, page 72

#155	Early, beaded buffalo design, excellent condition	$500 to $650
#156	Gosiute elk skin, floral beaded, good condition	$250 to $350
#157	Worn cowhide farriers' mittens	$35 to $65
#158	Left: long fringed, large floral design beading, fine	$300 to $400
#158	Right: Shorter cuffed, simple beading design, fine	$150 to $200
#159	Lady's cavalry gloves with Apache military motif beadwork	$250 to $300
#159	Right: Simple design, small Ute white buckskin gauntlets	$120 to $150

GUN RIGS, pages 75 and 76

#160	Pickard cantanas pommel bag holster	$850 to $1000
#160	Main and Winchester floral tooled pommel bags holster	$1700 to $1900
#161	Dragoon tarred flap holster	$200 to $275
#161	New Line kid-skin holster	$65 to $100
#161	1851 Navy buttoned flap holster	$125 to $200
#162	U.S. Model 1885 Colt or S&W military holster	$450 to $550
#163	California or Slim Jim holsters, carved, very good to excellent	$900 to $1500D
#164	Early, slim, Mexican loop holster, large rosette (scarce!)	$300 to $400
#164	Collins money/cartridge belt (early Wyoming maker)	$600 to $1200

GUN RIGS, continued pages 76 to 82

Photo #165	Early, edge tooled, Peacemaker Slim Jim (scarce)	$150 to $250
#165	Merwin and Bray 7½", three loop, lined holster	$500 to $600
#165	Short flap, tooled, double Mexican loop holster C.1890	$250 to $500
#166	Meanea 7½" S.A. holster, matched money/cartridge belt	$5000 to $6500
#167	32-20 money/cart. belt and double loop holster	$400 to $500
#167	38-40 money/cart belt, Rival holster with added studs	$450 to $550
#167	French 41 cal. combo, floral tooled holster (top quality!)	$1500 to $2000
#167	Texas jockstrap holster, 44 combo belt	$350 to $400
#167	Sears full tooled holster, 45 cal. money/cart. belt	$250 to $350
#168	Montgomery Wards holster, added spots and concho	$150 to $250
#168	Rival holster with added spots and concho	$200 to $300
#168	Shortened Gallup and Frazier holster (scarce maker mark)	$300 to $400
#169	Unmarked Texas pouch shoulder holster	$50 to $85
#169	Furstnow speed-draw shoulder holster	$75 to $125
#169	Visalia half-breed shoulder holster	$50 to $100
#170	Mail order Mexican loop for Lightning	$50 to $70
#170	Mail order pouch holster for Lightning (excellent)	$40 to $60
#171	Olive 6" D.A. holster	$75 to $100
#171	Olive 4¾" S.A. holster, (center) with combo belt	$250 to $400
#171	Shapleigh Diamond Brand shoulder holster	$45 to $75
#172	Donnel combo belt (well worn condition)	$450 to $650
#172	Mail order pouch holster (worn condition)	$25 to $35
#173	Heiser left hand, tooled, thong laced holster	$100 to $150
#173	Heiser full floral tooled, laced, S.A. holster (like new)	$400 to $475
#173	Heiser "Bull Head" holster with matching Heiser belta	$350 to $500
#174	Browning Bros small auto holsterb	$75 to $100
#174	Browning Bros. 7½" S.A. three loop holster, wide belt	$800 to $1400
#174	Browning Bros. laced single loop holster, narrower belt	$300 to $450
#175	Frazier money/cartridge belt (excellent)	$1000 to $1600
#175	Frazier full tooled single loop holster	$300 to $500
#175	Frazier tooled, double loop S.A. holster with snap strap	$150 to $200
#176	Sears tooled Cowboy holster and combo money belt	$500 to $650

#176	Lawrence pre-war matched S.A. rigi	$500 to $650
#177	Meldrum marked double loop holster only (rare!)	$1500 to $2000
#178	Farley and Franks single riveted loop, basket stamp	$200 to $350
#178	Mills dog-head pistol belt	$100 to $150
#179	Bridgeport rig on J.S. Collins money/cart belt (excellent)	$10,000 to $15,000
#180	Maestranza de Manila double loop holster, constabulary	$250 to $300
#180	Mueller 38 caliber cartridge belt	$150 to $225
#181	Mexican loop holster with art noveau nude	$90 to $125
#181	Flap auto holster with tooled cowboy	$90 to $135
#182	Various hip-pocket holsters (each)	$25 to $30
#183	Audley patent holster (holds trigger guard)	$25 to $30
#183	Clam shell holsters (spring open when pressed at trigger)	$60 to $80
#184	Tower single lock with barrel key	$120 to $150
#184	Bean/Cobb, patent 1899, with key	$120 to $165

HATS, page 85

#185	Wide brimmed plainsman	$600 to $1000
#185	Very high crowned "Big Boy"	$300 to $450
#186	Old soft felt cowboy hats, various makers, or unmarked	$75 to $150

HATS, pages 85 and 86, continued

Photo #187	Mexican sombrero, woven palm or other fiber	$50 to $125
#187	Stetson hat, 1940s	$25 to $50
#188	hair hat band	$350 to $550
#190	"Tom Mix" model Stetson (their biggest, near new)	$850 to $1250
#191	Various old or interesting Western hats	$25 to $60

HOBBLES, page 88

#192	Plain leather and chain buckle style	$20 to $35
#193	Mormon or trick hobbles (vary in quality and appeal)	$40 to $75

KNIVES, pages 91 and 92

#194	Wilkinson Shakespear knife and sheath (rare)	$1200 to $1800
#194	Booth, Sheffield Bowie, altered, replacement sheath	$1400 to $1700
#194	LF&C late Bowie, slab stag	$50 to $125
#194	Sioux beaded sheath c. 1900	$600 to $800
#195	Will and Finck camp	$1600 to $2500
#195	Knife	$35 to $60
#195	Knife and fork set	$40 to $65
#195	Fancy celluloid handled razor	$25 to $50
#196	Clip point Bowie hunter	$75 to $150
#196	Spear point Bowie hunter	$100 to $200
#196	Clip point Bowie hunter, worn	$40 to $75
#196	York ivory handled dagger	$250 to $400
#197	Antler handled dirk	$175 to $250
#197	Russell hunting/fishing knife, original sheath	$100 to $175
#197	Unmarked European dagger	$125 to $200
#198	John Bull Bowie, frontier replacement sheath	$250 to $350
#198	American Bowie hunter, nice sheath	$125 to $200
#198	German Bowie style hunter	$75 to $100
#198	Remington stacked leather handled hunter	$75 to $125
#199	London made large horseman's knife	$200 to $400
#199	New York Knife Co. large folder	$125 to $200
#199	Marbles Safety Axe Co. patented folder	$125 to $175
#199	Colonial folder, celluloid pearl handle	$20 to $40
#199	Early Case Tested folder, stag	$100 to $150

LOADING TOOLS, pages 94 and 95

#200	Early style (no groove) Colt dragoon mold (scarce)	$350 to $450
#200	Three various Colt bullet molds (each)	$60 to $100

#200	Percussion era round ball mold	$25 to $35
#201	Winchester molds and tools (each item)	$60 to $100
#202	Cast iron lead pot	$25 to $35
#203	Fairbanks early, fancy loading scale	$250 to $350
#203	Dupont #1 smokeless powder, clean full can	$100 to $150
#204	Shotgun reloading tool set	$100 to $150

NECKERCHIEFS, page 97
#205	1860s silk, (frayed)	$35 to $50
#206	Mexican Paisley pattern cotton	$10 to $25
#207	Silk rodeo motif, 1935	$60 to $125
#208	Pioneer Days, cotton, printed motif (1947)	$25 to $40

POKES, page 98
| Photo #209 | Apache beaded, 1880-1900 | $400 to $650 |

POWDER FLASKS AND HORNS, page 99
| #210 | Large powder horn (documented to 1850s) | $100 to $150 |
| #210 | Various powder and shot flasks | $60 to $150 |

QUIRTS, page 100
#211	Hitched tri-color horsehair	$100 to $150
#211	Modern Mexican braided rawhide	$25 to $40
#211.	Hamley six button braided rawhide, 1930	$100 to $150
#211	Old finely braided quality leather	$100 to $150
#211	Old, but cruder leather work	$25 to $50

REINS, page 102
#212	California style braided rawhide, average quality	$75 to $100
#213	Modern California reins and romal	$25 to $50
#214	Braided rawhide open reins	$50 to $75

ROPES AND REATAS, pages 104 to 106
#215	70' nice quality, used, Mexican reata	$150 to $250
#216	Very nice quality 80' American reata	$250 to $400
#217	reata	$125 to $200
#219	Wyoming or Colorado style, shorter, stronger reata	$150 to $300
#220	Black and white mane hair McCarty	$75 to $100
#221	Black 22' McCarty	$50 to $75
#222	Rodeo cowboy's tooled leather rope box	$100 to $250

SADDLES, pages 108 to 114
#223	Early half-seat trail saddle	$400 to $700
#224	G.H. & J.S. Collins Mother Hubbard (early and rare mark)	$4500 to $5000
#225	S.C. Gallup half-seat plains saddle	$900 to $1500
#226	Jenkins & Sons half-seat	$1000 to $1500
#227	Marks Bros. lighter stock saddle	$750 to $850
#228	Meanea 14P loop-seat cowboy saddle	$850 to $1250
#229	Frazier #196, silver horn, with bags	$800 to $1200
#230	Frazier #187 brass horn with "Pueblo" seat	$350 to $500
#231	Frazier special order Sam Stagg rigged saddle	$1000 to $1500
#232	Harris half-seat lady's astride saddle	$750 to $1200
#233	Thompson post-1900 Mother Hubbard	$1100 to $1600
#234	Flynn #170 stock saddle (excellent)	$750 to $1100
#235	Frazier very large "muley" saddle	$600 to $900
#236	Collins and Morrison swell fork	$350 to $500
#237	Horned plantation saddle	$250 to $500
#238	Capriola stock saddles (each)	$450 to $800
#239	RIA U.S. Model 1904 McClellan	$300 to $400
#239	U.S. 1904 saddle bags	$150 to $250

SADDLE BAGS, page 116

#240	Old with sheepskin cover	$75 to $125∂
#241	Wilson marked, small, c. 1900	$125 to $250
#241	U.S. 1904 saddle bags, liners	$150 to $250
#242	Bona Allen semi-modern	$25 to $75

SADDLE MAKER'S TOOLS, page 117

Photo #243	Quick measure gauge with maker's stamp	$75 t0 $100

SADDLE SCABBARDS, pages 119 to 120

#244	Early Slim Jim with vine, leaf carving (only fair cond)	$125 to $175
#2446	Full floral tooled early rifle, sewed round toe	$175 to $250
#245	Plain but early edge tooled carbine	$75 to $100
#245	Unmarked, early edge tooled large rifle size	$75 to $125
#246	Browning Bros. marked rifle scabbards (each)	$150 to $250
#247	Searle Saddlery, nice color, style and cartouche	$200 to $250
#247	Hand carved Slim Jim style	$150 to $225
#247	Brauer Bros. carbine size	$25 to $75
#247	Meanea edge tooled rifle scabbard	$400 to $800
#248	Bregenzer stamped scabbard, Probably a fake!!!	NOT PRICED
#248	Heiser #332 carbine scabbard	$75 to $150
#248	Western Saddle, edge tooled by hand	$50 to $125
#2499	Semi-modern Eubanks with some basket weave	$50 to $75
#24	N.L. Blair plain contoured rifle size	$75 to $150
#249	Utah prison deeply tooled, sheepskin lined	$40 to $65

SCALES, TONGUE OR HIDER'S, page 121

#250	Hand wrought hider's scale	$100 to $175

SKIRTS, RIDING, page 123

#251	Cotton skirt, leather fringed	$50 to $60
#251	Cotton riding skirt, plain	$20 to $30
#252	Hamley fancy kid-leather riding skirt	$800 to $1400

SPURS, pages 126 to 133

#253	Cast moccasin trade spurs	$50 to $100
#254	Buermann Eureka with original harness straps	$100 to $200
#255	Buermann OK spurs with original harness straps	$125 to $225
#256	Painted patent sheet metal spurs	$75 to $125
#257	Old and elaborate South American spurs	$250 to $350
#258	Mexican colonial or transitional	$250 to $450
#259	Large early Chihuahuas, plain	$100 to $250
#260	Fine quality inlaid Chihuahuas, Frazier straps	$400 to $800§
#261	Classic early California vaquero spurs, concho straps	$1200 to $1800
#262	Unmarked traditional California, made in Mexico c.1920s	$750 to $1000
#263	California with heart piercings, concho straps	$1250 to $1850
#264	G.S. Garcia #5 (variety of styles and variable quality, spurs with other Garcia marks less, watch for fakes)	$1200 to $1800
#265	Mike Morales, marked inside heel band	$2100 to $3000
#266	Morales with rounded M, heart motif silver	$2000 to $3500
#267	Silver bar inlaid Colorado style	$700 to $1000
#268	Large, heavy Schnitgers, big rowels, (unmarked)	$2800 to $3500
#269	Ed Hulbert silver and gold mounted, silver buckle straps	$2000 to $3000
#270	Ed Bohlin silver and gold mounted, silver concho straps	$2800 to $3500
#271	Buermann #1476 bar mounted California style	$1200 to $1600
#272	Buermann silver inlaid Roosevelt spurs	$3000 to $4500
#273	Buermann #1394 ½ Indian Chief	$450 to $650
#274	J.R. McChesney (unmarked) gal-legs	$500 to $650
#275	McChesney #1 Style L, twist shank, scarce mark	$500 to $600
#276	Big, inside marked McChesneys	$450 to $750

SPURS, continued, pages 134 to 144

Photo #277	Kelly Bros. Chihuahuas, diamond pattern mounting	$300 to $400
#278	C.P. Shipley gal-leg spurs	$800 to $1400
#279	Kelly Bros. Montana Joe style	$800 to $1200
#279	Kelly Bros. X-marked goose neck	$250 to $350
#280	KB&P with replaced rowels (hurts price)	$400 to $500
#281	Powder River large rowels, Chihuahua style	$300 to $350
#281	Powder River, chap guards, Texas style	$150 to $300
#282	Silver soldered stainless, concho straps	$75 to $125
#283	Early Canon City, bird head, hand filed rowels	$700 to $1000
#284	Frank Bradney prison spurs	$350 to $450
#285	Ricardo fully silver overlaid and engraved	$600 to $800
#286	Garcia silver overlayed with trophy inscription	$250 to $350
#287	Charles Wyatt big early bronc spurs	$75 to $175
#288	Frank Longtine arrow shank and concho	$400 to $650
#289	Buermann snow flake rowel spur	$250 to $400
#289	Crescent and cross motif, plated cast	$250 to $350
#290	Colonial style youth spurs, jeweled straps	$125 to $200
#291	Anchor Brand, drop shank, California	$125 to $200
#291	Anchor coarsely cast, plated	$35 to $65
#292	(Inside marked Crockett bull-heads	$750 to $1000
#293	1930s Colorado Specials	$150 to $225
#294	1930s Crockett bronc spurs	$100 to $175
#295	Burnished Crockett Denver Specials	$150 to $250
#295	Swing button blued mounted Crocketts	$200 to $275
#295	Crockett blued and mounted large roweled spurs	$450 tp $600
#296	Nickeled Crockett arrow shanks	$300 to $400
#296	Nickeled Crockett bottle openers	$300 to $400
#296	Crockett-Renalde dress spurs	$250 to $325
#297	Stainless Crocketts with bronze eagles	$250 to $350
#297	Nickeled Crocketts, plain with chap guards	$200 to $250
#297	Crockett bronc spurs with clover rowels	$100 to $150
#298	Kelly bull spurs #215, 1950s	$40 to $60
#298	Crockett blued elbow shank, silver mounted, 1960s	$75 to $85
#299	Blued and silver inlaid Mexican spurs	$100 to $200
#299	Engraved silver overlaid goose necks	$175 to $200
#300	Common U.S. Model 1911 spurs without rowels	$25 to $35
#300	Canadian military spurs	$25 to $35
#301	Brass U.S. Cavalry spurs, steel rowels, dated 1906	$60 to $90
#302	Blanchard roping spurs	$250 to $300
#303	Hall contemporary gal-legs	$150 to $225
#304	Modern contour fitted bronze spurs	$75 to $125
#305	Ranch forged gooseneck spurs	$50 to $70
#306	Giant shop made novelty spurs	$200 to $300
#307	Whittled wooden toy spurs	$10 to $15

STICKING TOMMY, page 145

#308	Very fancy, brass mounted, piercings	$300 to $600

STINGY GUNS, page 146

Photo #309	(from top left down) Colt open top 22	$300 to $375
#309	Engraved Colt open top 22	$350 to $500
#309	Nickeled Colt New Line 32	$250 to $350
#309	Blued Colt New Line 32	$250 to $350
#309	(from top right down) Colt Thuer 3rd Model Derringera	$250 to $350
#309	Engraved Colt New Line 22, pearl grips	$300 to $500
#309	Nickeled and rosewood Remington double Derringer	$300 to $600

STIRRUPS, page 148

#310	Cast ventilated iron stirrups	$45 to $65
#311	Old iron ring stirrups (each pair)	$35 to $45
#312	Silver inlaid brass Mexican stirrups	$75 to $125

TAPADEROS, page 150

#313	Simple shield type taps	$40 to $60
#314	Powder River bull dog taps	$40 to $80
#315	Long flowing taps	$100 to $200

WATCH FOBS, page 152

#316	Beaded watch case	$50 to $75
#316	Non-advertising watch fobs (each)	$20 to $40
#317	Pistol and holster fob	$40 to $60
#317	Wyoming Ranchman Outfitters fobs	$75 to $100
#317	R.T. Frazier, Pueblo, saddle fob	$125 to $175
#317	Hamley & Co., Pendleton "roundup" saddle fob	$125 to $200

WINCHESTERS, pages 154 to 157

As with Colts, variations and condition affect prices!

#318	Exceptional New England half-stock rifle	$1500 to $2000
#318	Winchester Model 1866 octagon rifle	$3000 to $4000
#318	Model 1873 octagon rifle	$450 to $650
#318	Model 1876 octagon rifle	$1000 to $1600
#319	Model 1885 Special Sporting Rifle	$800 to $1000
#319	Model 1886 octagon rifle	$1600 to $1900
#319	Model 1895 round rifle	$650 to $850
#320	Model 1890 octagon rifles (top and bottom, each)	$200 to $350
#320	Model 1906 pump rifle	$200 to $300
#321	Model 1892 round barrel rifle	$550 to $650
#321	Model 1892 Deluxe Take-Down rifle	$1200 to $1600
#321	Model 1892 octagon rifle	$750 to $1000
#322	Model 1894 octagon rifle	$500 to $700
#322	Model 1894 octagon short rifle	$1500 to $2200
#322	Model 1894 round barrel rifle	$350 to $450
#323	Model 1866 carbine	$3000 to $4500
#323	Model 1895 carbine	$900 to $1200
#324	Winchester 1873 carbine (only)	$750 to $900
#325	Model 1893 pump shotgun	$400 to $600
#325	Model 1887 lever shotgun	$350 to $550
#326	Model 1885 octagon rifle	$400 to $600
#326	Model 1886 special order octagon rifle	$3500 to $4500
#327	Model 1885 short rifle (one-of-a-kind)	RARE

INDEX OF MAKERS

ABERCROMBIE & FITCH CO.
New York, San Francisco, Chicago
Large sporting goods dealer and safari outfitter. Absorbed Von Lengerke & Antoine, Chicago. Catalogs, Photo 105

ALLEGHENY ARSENAL; Pennsylvania
Mark on Model 1859 U.S. bit. Bits, Photo 29.

ALLEN, BONA; Buford, Georgia
Established in 1873. Saddle Bags, Photo 242.

ALLEN, JOSEPH (later Jospeh Allen & Sons,
NON XLL brand) Sheffield, England, 1864-1947
Located at Oak Works, New Edwards Street until 1889, then at Ecclesall Works, Rockingham Street. Knives, Photo 196.

ANCHOR BRAND
(or anchor mark on bits, spurs, harness hardware, belt buckles, and snaps); a trademark of North and Judd Mfg. Co.

ANDREW, R. J. (Concho Brand saddles);
San Angelo, Texas. Catalogs, Photo 91.

AUDLEY PATENT, Oct. 13, 1914.
Patent granted to Francis H. Audley, New York, covering locking device in holsters that were manufactured by H. & D. Folsom Arms Co., 314 Broadway, New York , circa 1920. Gun Rigs, Photo 183.

B.G.I. CO.
See Bridgeport Gun Implement Co.

BEAN OR BEAN-COBB HANDCUFFS
Handcuffs, Photo 184.

BENICIA ARSENAL; California
Mark on Model 1874 U.S. Saber belt. Gun Rigs, Photo 163.

BLAIR, N.L.; Pinedale, Wyoming
Contemporary saddle maker now at Cheyenne, Wyoming. Saddle Scabbards, Photo 249.

BLANCHARD, E.F.; Yucca, Arizona
(and other locations)
Recently-deceased maker of nice-quality cutting horse and roping-style spurs. Spurs, Photo 302.

BOHLIN, EDWARD H.; Hollywood, California
Saddle maker and silversmith most associated with fine parade equipment. A Swedish emigrant at 17, he was a cowboy, acquaintance of Buffalo Bill, and worked in the movies. Business has existed 1922 to present. Catalogs, Photo 98. Spurs, Photo 270.

BOOTH, H. (enry) C.(arr); Sheffield, England
Operated small cutlery factory titled Norfolk Works, Norfolk Lane, Sheffield   C. 1852-1876. Knives, Photo 194.

BRADNEY, FRANK B.; Canon City, Colorado
Spur maker at prison. 1934-1964 spurs marked *By F.B.*; began numbering spurs in 1964. Most spurs are mounted with nickel alloy and 2-karat Dixie gold. Spurs, Photo 284.

BRAUER BROS. MFG. CO.
(also Moose Brand); St. Louis, Missouri
Semi-modern to contemporary maker of mass-produced gun leather. Saddle Scabbards, Photo 247.

BREGENZER, F(rank) J.; Rifle, Colorado
Manager and later owner of the W.R. Thompson shop in Rifle. Afterward had a shop of his own name. C. 1917. Cuffs, Photo 145. Saddle, page vi. Saddle Scabbards, Photo 248. Picture this section.

BRIDGEPORT GUN IMPLEMENT CO.;
Bridgeport, Connecticut
Manufacturers of numerous gun accoutrements, including the rare and valuable "Bridgeport rig," a fast-draw rig patented by L.S. Flatau, No. 252448, Jan. 17, 1882. Gun Rigs, Photo 179 Loading Tools, Photo 204.

BRINGHAM PATENT
Mark frequently seen on older cartridge belts with a laced-through loop design. Reportedly dates from 1890s.
Belts, Photo 10.

BROWNING BROS.; Ogden, Utah
(or, infrequently, Salt Lake City)
Manufactured John Browning-patent, single-shot rifle, 1879 to 1883. In wholesale, retail, and mail-order sporting-goods business at Ogden 1883-1926 and in Salt Lake 1898-1901. Catalogs, Photo 104. Gun Rigs, Photo 174. Saddle Scabbards, Photo 246. Winchesters, Photo 319.

Frank J. Bregenzer (in apron) poses in his Rifle, Colorado, saddle shop with William Grigor, owner of the G+ ranch, c. 1917.

BUERMANN, AUGUST (Star Brand bits and spurs)
Newark, New Jersey
Established in 1842 and acquired by North and Judd 1920. Once the largest manufacturer of bits and spurs in the world. Marks include a star with the initials A.B. inside and superimposed, OK, Eureka, Star Steel Silver, Hercules Bronze, and very frequent use of the word patented or the contraction PAT'D on bits and spurs. Bits, Photos 18, 20, 22, 23, 24, 25, 31, 33. Catalogs, Photo 109. Spurs., Photos 254, 255, 271, 272, 273, 289.

BULL, JOHN; Sheffield, England
Trademark registered to Rodgers Brothers.

BUNN, HENRY AND SAM; Rifle, Colorado.
Amateur spur makers in area of Divide Creek 1930s. Spurs, Photo 306.

BY F.B.
Spur maker's mark of Frank Bradney.

C.R. (Superimposed in a horse shoe).
Spur mark of Crockett and Renalde, Denver, Colorado.

CAPRIOLA, J(oe) M.; Elko, Nevada.
Saddle maker employed by G.S. Garcia. Established own firm in 1929. Operated by son, Joe Jr. until his death in 1947, by Frank Jayo 1955 to 1958, and by the Paul Bear family since October of 1958. Acquired the Garcia business (imported Mexican spurs) about 1978 from Les Garcia. Catalogs, Photo 100. Saddles, Photo 238.

CASE, W.R. (Also Case Bros., Case Tested XX)
Gowanda, Springville, and Little Valley, New York. Under various names, cutlery makers since 1889. Case Tested marks after 1903. Large C trademark generally prior to 1940. Knives, Photo 199.

CHICAGO HIDE, FUR & WOOL HOUSE; Douglas, Wyoming
Coats, Photos 123, 124.

CHILDS, S.D. & CO.; Chicago
Badges, Photo 5.

CHORNHILL; London, England
Knives, Photo 199.

CLAMSHELL
Trademark of Stanroy Mfg. Co. and later C.A. Hoffman & Sons.

CLAUBERG CUTLERY CO.; Solingen, Germany
1857 - Present. Knives, Photo 198.

COGSHALL, C.E.
Miles City, Montana businessman who acquired Hugh Moran shop in 1895, formed partnership with Al Furstnow by 1897, sold out to Miles City Saddlery (who continued to catalog *Original Cogshall Saddles*) in 1909. Catalogs, Photo 89. Chaps, Photo 116.

COLLINS, G.H. & J.S. (1876-1880)
J.S. Collins (1880-1885); J.S. Collins & Co. (1886-1890), Cheyenne, Wyoming; and (J.S.) Collins and (John) Morrison, Omaha,
Nebraska. John S. Collins was appointed by family friend, President U.S. Grant as post trader, Ft. Laramie, Wyoming Territory. First saddle shop was with brother, Gilbert, in Omaha, 1864. Gilbert committed suicide in Cheyenne in 1880. John reorganized in 1881, and again with a new partner, John Morrison, in 1886. Returned to Omaha about 1890, where he died in 1910. Gun Rigs, Photos 164, 179. Saddles, Photos 224, 236.

COLONIAL; Providence, Rhode Island
(1926-Present) Cutlery firm established by Paolantonio brothers at 19 Calendar Street. Knives, Photo 199.

COLORADO SADDLERY CO.; Denver, Colorado
Contemporary saddlers. Catalogs, Photo 100.

COLORADO STATE PRISON; Canon City, Colorado
Bridles, Photos 74, 75. Spurs, Photos 283, 284 and page vi.

COLTS PATENT FIRE ARMS CO.; Hartford, Connecticut
Previously Patent Arms Mfg. Co., Paterson, New Jersey, 1836-1840. Whitneyville, Connecticut, 1847. (New York and London addresses were also used.) Advertising, Photo 1. Colts, All Photos. Gun Rigs, All Photos. Loading Tools, Photo 200. Stingy Guns, Photo 309.

CONCHO SADDLES
Trademark of R.J. Andrew: San Angelo, Texas.

CROCKETT, O(scar)
Later Crockett, and in 1950s Crockett and Renalde. Started as a blacksmith about 1910 in Kansas City. Owned shop at Pawhuska, Oklahoma in 1916. Joined Chas P. Shipley, whose spur business he acquired about 1932 and moved to Lenexa, Kansas. Moved to Boulder, Colorado, in 1943 and died in 1949. Business acquired in 1950s by Jim Renalde. Operated erratically until 1985. Bits, Photos 34, 47. Catalogs, Photo 109. Spurs, Photos 292, 293, 294, 295, 296, 297, 298.

D.F.B. CO. (Gopher Brand)
Dodson, Fisher, Brockman Co., Minneapolis, Minnesota. Cuffs, Photo 147.

DENVER DRY GOODS CO; Denver, Colorado
(Powder River brand) Large department store that continued operation until 1986. Saddle and tack manufacture and sales diminished after World War II. Catalogs, Photos 96, 97. Spurs, Photo 281. Tapaderos, Photo 314.

DIAMOND BRAND
Trademark of Shapleigh Hardware (and various partnerships), 1864-1960.

DONNEL, J.A.; Rawlins, Wyoming
Saddler born July 17, 1845, in Mottville, N.Y. Was a Union Army veteran, Western adventurer. Established a ranch and a Rawlins saddle shop by 1880. Died in 1918. Catalogs, Photo 88. Gun Rigs, Photo 172. Photograph in this section.

EH
(applied with small, slightly curved lines, not a full stamp). Spurmaker's mark of Ed C. Hulbert

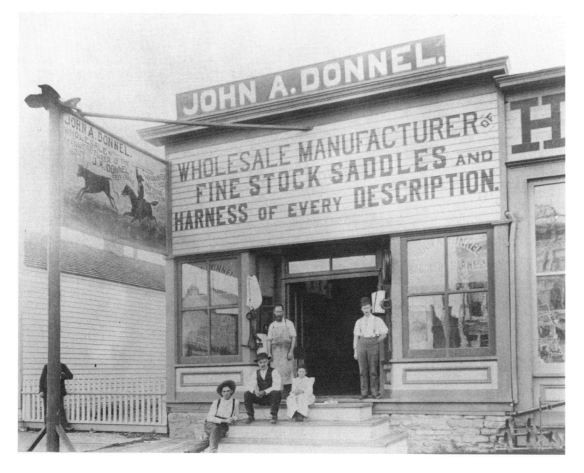

The John A. Donnell saddle shop in Rawlins, Wyoming Territory, about 1880. Identities of the individuals pictured are unknown.

EUBANKS LEATHER; Boise, Idaho
(also Pioneer Leather). Semi-modern manufacturer of gun leather. Saddle Scabbards, Photo 249.

FAIRBANKS SCALES
Loading Tools, Photo 203.

FARLEY & FRANKS; The Dalles, Oregon
Semi-modern maker of gun leather. Gun Rigs, Photo 178.

FLYNN, T. (om); Pueblo, Colorado
Major saddler who operated at Silver Cliff, Colorado, in the 1880s and at Pueblo from 1889 until his death in 1921. Shop continued by his son, Frank, until 1935. Cuffs, Photo 154. Saddles, Photo 234.

FOLSOM, H.D. CO.; New York
Manufacturers of Audley patent holsters. Catalogs, Photo 105. Gun Rigs, Photo 183.

FRANKLIN, O.M. SERUM CO.
Branding Irons, Photo 68.

FRAZIER, R.(obert) T.; Pueblo, Colorado
One of the big names and, at one time, the largest manufacturer of Western stock saddles. Worked for P. Becker at Leadville, then S.C. Gallup in Pueblo, where he became first a partner and then acquired the saddlery in 1897. He died in 1931. The company survived into the mid-1940s. Catalogs, Photo 89. Chaps, page vi. Cuffs, Photo 143. Gun Rigs, Photo 175. Saddles, Photo 229, 230, 231, 235. Spurs, Photo 260. Watch Fobs, Photo 317.

FRENCH, M.E.; Montrose, Colorado
Successor to Chas. Swope Saddlery until 1911. Gun Rigs, Photo 167.

FURSTNOW, AL(bert F.); Miles City, Montana
Saddlemaker who was born in Fond du Lac, Wisconsin, in 1862. He was a foreman for G.H. & J.S. Collins at Cheyenne. Worked in Miles City in 1884 and opened his own shop there in 1894. He was in partnership with Cogshall in the late 1890s, died in 1923, and his shop was owned and operated by a man named Moreno by the 1930s. Chaps, Photo 120, Gun Rigs, Photo 169.

GALLUP & SONS; Denver, Colorado
Belts, Photo 14.

GALLUP, S.C.; Pueblo, Colorado
Early saddle-maker, 1870s, who was the younger brother of Francis Gallup, saddler of Denver. He sold out to R.T. Frazier in 1897 after some years of partnership and established the S.C. Gallup Saddlery Co. across the street in 1898. He died about 1900, but the shop continued until 1930. Chaps, Photo 113. Saddles, Photo 225.

GALLUP, S.C. AND FRAZIER; Pueblo, Colorado
Very desirable maker's mark from the 1890s partnership of these two prominent saddle-makers. Gun Rigs, Photo 168.

GARCIA; Reno, Nevada
Previously Garcia Saddlery Co., Salinas California. Founded at Salinas in 1936, when Les and Henry Garcia moved the shop of their late father, G.S. Garcia, from Elko, Nevada. Closed during WWII, the shop was reopened from 1946 to 1957. Les Garcia, living at Reno, Nevada, continued the import of Mexican bits and spurs until this business was sold to J.M. Capriola Co. at Elko in 1978. Bits, Photo 47. Catalogs, Photo 98. Spurs, Photo 286.

GARCIA, G.(audalupe) S.; Elko, Nevada
A native of Mexico, this famous leather-worker began a shop in Santa Margarita, California, about 1885 and moved to Elko, Nevada, in 1894. He employed many notable bit and spur makers from 1896 until 1932, when the business was taken over by his sons, Les and Henry. Spurs, Photo 264.

GARCIA SADDLERY; see Garcia, Reno Nevada

GLOBE TANNING CO.; Des Moines, Iowa
Tannery and manufacturer of fur garments and robes. Coats, Photo 124.

GOPHER BRAND;
A trademark of the D.F.B. Company

GORDON & FERGUSON; St. Paul, Minnesota
Coats, Photo 122.

GREEN RIVER
A trademark of J. Russell & Company

HALL
Spur maker's mark of contemporary spur maker, Carl Hall, Commanche, Texas, who makes spurs and bits of old styles. Bits, Photo 37. Spurs, Photo 303.

HAMLEY AND COMPANY; Pendleton, Oregon
(also Circle H Brand). Large and successful saddlery begun at Ashton, South Dakota in 1883, moved to Kendrick, Idaho, in 1890, and to Pendleton, Oregon, about 1905. Long associated with the famous Pendleton Roundup Rodeo, which began in 1910, and development of the early "Committee" and "Association" standardized bronc-riding saddles. Catalogs, Photos 91, 92, 93. Chaps, Photo 121. Quirts, Photo 211. Skirts, Photo 252. Watch Fobs, Photo 317.

HAMMER BRAND
The trademark of New York Knife Co. (Later used by Imperial Cutlery after 1935).

HARRIS, J.G.; Greely, Colorado
Saddles, Photo 232.

HEISER, HERMAN H.; Denver, Colorado
(also three H's in various configurations). Major saddler and gun-leather manufacturing plant founded in Denver in 1874 at the location of the old Gallatin and Gallup shop. Herman Heiser, a German immigrant, had been a book-binder in Wisconsin about 1858 when company catalogs dated the founding of the business. Merged with Keyston about 1950. Catalogs, Photos 95, 100, 101. Chaps, Photos 112, 115. Cuffs, Photo 144. Gun Rigs, Photos 173, 174, 175 and page vi.. Saddle Scabbards, Photos 246, 248.

HI-GLO
Badges, Photo 4.

HOFFMAN, C.A. & SONS MFGRS.; Arlington, California
(Clamshell) Gun Rigs, Photo 183.

HULBERT, ED. C.; Kane, Wyoming
(Spurs marked E.H. with small, slightly curved die). Made fine-quality, silver-mounted spurs that were retailed by Otto Ernst, Sheridan, and Hamley, Pendleton, in the 1920s and early 1930s. Spurs, Photo 269.

I*XL
Trademark of George Wostenholm & Son on cutlery.

JENKINS AND SONS, Also J.W. Jenkins: Salt Lake City, UT
Founded by J.W. Jenkins Sr. in 1855. J.W. Jenkins Jr. ran the shop from 1890 until 1940, and J.W. Jenkins III from 1940 until 1973. Saddles, Photo 226.

K.B. & P. or Kelly marks on bits and spurs; see Kelly Bros.
KELLY BROS. MANUFACTURERS; El Paso, Texas
(also spurs marked X or O by the buttons.) P.M. Kelly began spur-making at Childress, Texas, in 1903, later at Hausford, Texas. He worked for J.R. McChesney about 1910. He opened another plant at Dalhart, Texas, and finally moved it to El Paso, Texas. K.B. & P. marked spurs were made during the period that Clyde Parker was a partner in the firm, and the latest spurs were marked only *Kelly* or *Rodeo*. The firm was acquired by Jim Renalde about 1965. Bits, Photo 36. Catalogs, Photo 109. Spurs, Photos 277, 279, 280, 298.

KEYSTON BROS; San Francisco
Originally whip makers, the firm was founded in 1868 by James Keyston, son of a Main & Winchester foreman. He was joined by his brother, William, in 1872. The company acquired the J.C. Johnson and L.D. Stone saddlery by 1912, H.H. Heiser in 1950, and Lichtenberger-Ferguson in 1959. Belts, Photo 12.

KIRKENDALL, Omaha, Nebraska
Boots, Photo 65.

L.F. & C. or LANDERS, FRARY & CLARK;
New Britain, Connecticut
Incorporated in 1865, this became the largest cutlery producer in the world by 1903. Produced much military equipment and closed in 1950. Knives, Photo 194.

LAMPHERE, BILL; Bountiful, Utah
Previously Scotts Bluff, Nebraska. Spurs, Photo 282.

LANZ, OWEN & CO.; Chicago, Illinois
Gun Rigs, Photo 162.

LAWRENCE, GEORGE & CO.; Portland, Oregon
Originally established in 1857 by Samuel Sherlock, the shop was acquired by George Lawrence and the name changed in 1893. Originally manufacturers of saddles and tack, they manufactured primarily gun leather after WW II. The business was continued by Bill Lawrence into the 1980s. Belts, Photos 10, 14. Catalogs, Photo 99. Chaps, Photo 118. Gun Rigs, Photo 176.

LEFEVRE, GEORGE; Meeker, Colorado
Boots (spurs), Photo 67.

LONGTINE, FRANK SR.; Riverton and Big Sandy, Wyoming
Spurs, Photo 288.

M, OR MM (with rounded appearance)
Mark on silver-inlaid bits and spurs. Maker mark of Mike Morales.

M & B CO.
Entwined in leather cartouche. See Merwin and Bray Co.

MAESTRANZA DE MANILA
Or the Armory of Manila was a U.S. depot during the Philippine Insurrections, 1898 to 1902, and for some years following. Gun Rigs, Photo 180.

MAIN & WINCHESTER; San Francisco, California
An early and major northern California saddlery from 1849 until acquired by Keyston Bros. in 1912. The firm was founded by Charles Main and E.H. Winchester and was consolidated with the L.D. Stone Company in 1905. Gun Rigs, Photo 160.

MARBLE SAFETY AXE CO., later Marble Arms & Manufacturing Co.; Gladstone, Michigan
Established in 1898 by W.L. Marble, who had invented a folding pocket-axe and a waterproof match safe. Name was changed in 1911. Folding hunting knives were made from 1900 until 1942. Knives, Photo 199.

MARDEN, VICTOR; The Dalles, Oregon.
Quality saddler who established his firm about 1890. Catalogs, Photo 89. Chaps, Photo 110.

MARKS BROS.; Omaha, Nebraska
Saddles, Photo 227.

MATSON, AL; Redding, California
Boots (spurs), Photo 6.

MCCHESNEY, JOHN ROBERT
Bit and spur maker of great reputation born at South Bend, Indiana, in 1867. Began making spurs about 1887 in Broken Arrow, Oklahoma. He moved to Gainesville, Texas, in 1890 and to Pauls Valley, Oklahoma, in 1910. There he employed as many as fifty men in the manufacture of spurs and bits. The business was acquired after McChesney's death in 1928, by Enid Justin of Nocona Boot Company, and the manufacture of spurs marked *McChesney* was begun. Earlier spurs were unmarked or, infrequently, have an arm-and-hammer imprint. Bits, Photo 36. Spurs, Photos 274, 275, 276.

MEANEA F.(rank) A.; Cheyenne, Wyoming
A nephew of E.L. Gallatin, Frank Meanea began as a manager of the Gallup and Gallatin shop in 1868, acquired it in the 1870s, and changed the shop name by 1881. He was a careful craftsman and successful merchandiser, and his Cheyenne shop became popular with cowboys of the Northern Plains and is very much so with modern collectors. He used exclusively saddletrees made by his brother, Theodore Meanea, of Denver until 1920. He died in 1928. Chaps, Photo 114. Gun Rigs, Photo 166.

Holster, front cover. Saddles, Photo 228. Saddle Scabbards, Photo 247.

MELDRUM, BOB; Rawlins, Wyoming
To "Bad Man" Bob Meldrum, saddle-making was just a side-line. He worked variously as a stock detective, strike-breaker, lawman, and killer. He was ultimately imprisoned for the killing of Baggs, Wyoming, cowboy Chick Bowen while Meldrum was town marshal of that community. After serving from 1916 to 1921 in the Wyoming State Penitentiary, he established a saddlery at Walcott, Wyoming. He disappeared mysteriously in the early 1920s, along with the money of the investors who had befriended him. Gun Rigs, Photo 177.

MERWIN & BRAY CO.; Worcester, Massachusetts, and New York City
Large pre-1900 sporting-goods jobbers whose holsters are marked with an entwined M. and B. Co. Gun Rigs, Photo 165.

MESSING, H. & SON; San Jose, California
Bits, Photo 21.

MILES CITY SADDLERY CO.; Miles City, Montana
Successor in 1909 to the Cogshall Saddle Co., they continued to market this line as "The Original Cogshall Saddles." Catalogs, Photo 89. Chaps, Photo 116.

MILLER RIDING EQUIPMENT (Stockman-Farmer); Denver, Colorado
Catalogs, Photos 96, 97.

MILLER, BLAKE; Cheyene, Wyoming
Operated a saddlery at Cheyenne from 1915 to 1927. Later worked in Denver. Catalogs, Photo 89.

MILLS, ANSON OR MILLS & ORNDORFF (T.C.) Worcester, Massachusetts
General Anson Mills, a famous Indian War-campaigner, designed and patented a leather military cartridge-belt at Fort Bridger, Wyoming, in 1866. He later designed and manufactured a woven-web belt and other military and civilian accoutrements. Belts, Photo 9. Gun Rigs, Photos 162, 177. Winchesters, Photos 324, 326.

MONTGOMERY WARD & CO.; Chicago, Illinois
Bits, Photo 23. Gun Rigs, Photo 168.

MOOSE BRAND
See Bauer Bros. Mfg. Co.

MORALES, MIKE (rounded M or MM trademark) Pendleton and Portland, Oregon, and Los Angeles, California
Morales worked several years with the G.S. Garcia firm in Elko, then moved to Pendleton, where he opened a shop with Hamley & Co. in 1910. He established his own company at Portland by 1920 and moved it to Los Angeles in 1927. Bits, Photo 26. Catalogs, Photo 108. Spurs, Photos 265, 266.

MUELLER, FRED; Denver, Colorado
Established quality saddle shop in Denver in 1883 and ran it until 1917. Company continued through 1940s. Catalogs, Photos 96, 97. Gun Rigs, Photo 180.

MYRES, S.D. (Tio Sam) El Paso, Texas
Started saddlery at Sweetwater, Texas, in 1897, and the business survived his death into the 1980s. Most noted for fine semi-modern gun rigs and, like Heiser, published separate gun-leather catalogs. Catalogs, Photo 102.

NEW YORK KNIFE CO.: Walden, New York (Hammer Brand)
Cutlery firm established originally at Mattewan, New York, in 1850, moved to Walden in 1856, and remained in business until 1931. The famous "Hammer Brand" with an arm and hammer was adopted in about 1880 and was acquired by Imperial Knife Co. in 1936. Knives, Photo 199.

NOCONA BOOT CO.; Nocona, Texas
Major boot-making firm founded by Enid Justin. She also acquired the J.R. McChesney bit-and-spur plant in 1928 and began the manufacture of those bits and spurs that are actually marked *McChesney*. Catalogs, Photo 106. Spurs, Photo 276.

NON XLL
Cutlery trademark of Joseph Allen, Sheffield, England.

NORTH AND JUDD MFG. CO; New Britian, Connecticut
(Anchor Brand and after 1920, Star Brand.) Large manufacturer of mass-produced bits, spurs, and harness hardware. Acquired the August Buermann Co. (Star Brand) about 1920 and continued manufacture of many of their styles, usually marked with a star lacking the A.B. initials and occasionally marked with both star and anchor. Bits, Photo 40, 46. Catalogs, Photo 108, Spurs, Photo 291.

O
Spur mark of Kelly Bros.

OLIVE OR OLIVE PATENT
Mark on holsters probably used by Shapleigh Hardware. Gun Rigs, Photo 171.

OXFORD, GERMANY
Cutlery mark of Germania Cutlery Works. Knives, Photo 195.

PATRICK MOISE KLINKNER CO.; San Francisco, California
Badges, Photo 4.

PAWNEE BILLS INDIAN TRADING POST; Pawnee, Oklahoma
Post-1900 tourist museum, buffalo ranch, and retail and wholesale house for Indian beadwork. Owned by Ray O. Lyon and Gordon W. Lillie (Pawnee Bill). Catalogs, Photo 90.

PICKARD, W.L. & SONS; Salt Lake City, Utah
General saddlers c. 1870 to 1885. Succeeded by Wallin and Pickard. Gun Rigs, Photo 160.

PORTER, N.(ewton); Phoenix, Arizona
Early Texas saddler who was located at Tharall, Taylorville, and Abilene, Texas, between 1875 and 1885. Moved to Seattle, Washington, and finally to Phoenix in 1895. Died in 1906. The business was managed by son, Earl, until 1925, and then by F.S. Porter. Swastikas were used extensively by Porters until about 1933, and they may have been the source of items with swastika-adorned snaps. They later used a steer-head trademark. Catalogs, Photos 92, 94, 98. Cuffs, Photo 151.

POSADA, DAVID , BOOTMAKER; Hollywood, California
Maker of fine-quality cowboy boots. His 1932 catalog states, "Seventeen years in the West." Catalogs, Photo 106.

POWDER RIVER, on saddles and spurs.
Trademark of Denver Dry Goods Co.

R.I.A. Mark of Rock Island Arsenal.

READ, J.G. & BROS.; Ogden, Utah
Acquired Hodgman Saddlery in 1883 and existed about 100 years. Used the controversial "Nigger Boy Brand" for several years. Nigger Boy was a famous harness race horse owned by the Reads. Catalogs, Photo 92.

REMINGTON, ELIPHALET Remington Arms Co. (1886-1912), and Remington-U.M.C. (1912-1934); Ilion, New York
Founded in 1816 and the oldest extant firearms manufacturers in the U.S. They also manufactured cutlery at Bridgeport, Connecticut from 1915 to 1940. Cartridges, Photos 85, 86, 87. Knives, Photos 198. Stingy Guns, Photo 309.

RENALDE, JIM; Denver, Colorado
Maker of primarily aluminum spurs in the 1940s; acquired Crockett and Kelly firms.

RICARDO, DON; Denver Colorado
Cataloged from the late 1930s through early 1950s. Ricardo manufactured nice quality, semi-modern spurs, bits, and engraved silver buckles and adornments. Boots (spurs), Photo 63. Spurs, Photo 285.

RIVAL (Holsters)
Gun Rigs, Photos 167, 168.

ROBERTS, JOE; Maybell, Colorado
Ropes, Photo 220.

ROCK ISLAND ARSENAL; Illinois
Bits, Photo 30. Saddles, Photo 239. Spurs, Photo 301.

RODEO
Spur mark of Kelly Spur Co.

RODGERS BROS.; SHEFFIELD, ENGLAND (John Bull)
Knives, Photo 198.

ROSLERS - NACHFOLGER; Austria
Knives, Photo 197.

**RUSSELL, J. & CO.; Green River Works.
Turner Falls, Massachusetts**
Founded in 1834. Makers of the famous Green River skinning and hunting knives. Early knives are stamped *J. Russell & Co. Green River Works* in two lines. Later a diamond was added and, even later, the 1834 date. Knives, Photos 195, 197.

RUWART MANUFACTURING CO.; Denver, Colorado
Catalogs, Photo 100.

SACHS-LAWLOR, Denver, Colorado
Badges, Photo 5.

SALT LAKE STAMP CO.
Badges, Photos 4, 5, 6, 7.

SAN ANGELO EASY STOP
Bits, Photo 49.

SCHNITKER, REX; Gillette, Wyoming
Maker of unmarked, but distinguishable Northern Plains-style spurs. c 1920s. Spurs, Photo 268.

SEARLE SADDLERY; Vernal, Utah
Saddle Scabbards, Photo 247.

SEARS ROEBUCK & CO.; Chicago, Illinois
Bits, Photo 23. Gun Rigs, Photos 167, 176. Hats, Photo 185. Skirts (blouse), Photo 251.

SHAKESPEAR KNIFE. see Wilkinson Sword Co.

SHAPLEIGH HARDWARE CO.; St. Louis, Missouri
(Diamond Brand) Founded in 1843 by A.F. Shapleigh, the firm continued business with some name variations until 1960. Gun Rigs, Photos 171, 182.

SHIPLEY, C.(harles) P.; Kansas City, Missouri
Founded in 1884 and continued business into the 1960s. Primarily saddlers, the company was involved in bit and spur manufacture with Oscar Crockett and sold McChesney spurs with a stamped arm-and-hammer within a diamond trademark. Catalogs, Photo 98. Spurs, Photo 278.

SNYDER, O.J. and SNYDER SADDLES; Denver, Colorado
Chaps, Photo 117. Cuffs, Photo 146.

STANROY MANUFACTURING CO; Bakersfield, California
(Clam Shell) Gun Rigs, Photo 183.

STERN'S; San Jose, California
Catalogs, Photo 99.

STETSON, J.(ohn) B. CO.; Philadelphia, Pennsylvania
Premier manufacturer of cowboy hats, the firm was founded in 1865. Re-organized in the 1980s, they continue to manufacture several early styles. Catalogs, Photo 96. Hats, Photos 187, 188, 189, 190, 191.

STOCKMAN-FARMER SUPPLY CO.
See Miller Riding Equipment

STRONG CURIO CO.; Gordon, Nebraska
Successors to (Ray O.) Lyon & Strong, the new partnership included noted Indian photographer James A. Miller. Their 1915 catalog lists full-beaded and quilled Sioux pipe-bags for five to eight dollars. Catalogs, Photo 90.

THOMPSON, W.R.; Rifle, Colorado
A major Western Slope saddlery firm founded in 1888. Thompson died in 1908, but the business continued under the management of Kirchner, Bregenzer, Dougan and was finally closed on the death of Ed Webb in 1941. Saddles, Photo 233. Saddle Maker's Tools, Photo 243.

THOMSON & SON; New York
Catalogs, Photo 103.

TOWER HANDCUFFS
Handcuffs, Photo 184.

U.S. ARSENALS
See Benicia, Rock Island, Watervliet.

UTAH STATE PRISON; Sugarhouse (now at Draper), Utah
Badges, Photo 6. Saddle Scabbards, Photo 249.

VISALIA STOCK SADDLE CO.; San Francisco, California
(D.E. Walker) Major saddlery firm founded at Visalia, California, in 1870 by Henry G. Shuham and David E. Walker. It was acquired and moved to San Francisco by Edmond W. Weeks in 1899 but continued to use the famous D.E. Walker trade name. The firm was acquired by Kenway Saddle Co. of Calgary, Canada, in the late 1950s. Advertising, Photo 3. Catalogs, Photos 91, 92, 98, 99. Gun Rigs, Photo 169.

WALKER, D.(avid) E. and various partners
See Visalia Stock Saddle Co.

WATERVLIET ARSENAL
Belts, Photo 9.

**WESTERN ARMS AND SPORTING GOODS CO;
Salt Lake City, Utah**
Catalogs, Photo 105.

WESTERN CARTRIDGE CO.
Cartridges, Photos 85, 87. Colts, Photo 133.

WESTERN SADDLE MFG. CO.; Denver, Colorado
(J.H. Wilson) Successors in 1919 to J.H. Wilson saddlery, founded in 1885, and continued to use the trade name into the 1930s. Catalogs, Photo 95. Saddle Scabbards, Photo 248.

WHITE & DAVIS; Pueblo, Colorado
Retail and mail-order firm of the 'teens to 1930s who marketed Heiser-manufactured leather goods under their trademark. Catalogs, Photo 96. Gun Rigs, Photo 175.

WILKINSON SWORD CO.; London, England
(Shakespear Knife) Cutlers since 1772 who manufactured the Shakespear knife in the mid-1800s. Knives, Photo 194.

WILL & FINCK; San Francisco, California
Partnership of Frederick Will and Julius Finck founded in 1863. Famous as makers of Bowie knives, push daggers, and the developers of the California Camp knife. Name used until 1932. Knives, Photo 195.

WILSON, GEORGE C.; Delta, Colorado
Saddle Bags, Photo 241.

WILSON, J.H.; Denver, Colorado
See Western Saddle Co.

WINCHESTER, OLIVER F. and WINCHESTER REPEATING ARMS CO.; New Haven, Connecticut
Winchester, a textile manufacturer and owner of the predecessor New Haven Arms Co., renamed the firm in 1866. Belts, Photo 9. Cartridges, Photos 85, 86, 87. Loading Tools, Photo 201. Winchesters, all photos.

WOSTENHOLM, GEORGE & SON; Sheffield, England (I*XL)
Founded c. 1745 at Stannington, moved to Rockingham Works, Sheffield, in 1832, and to Washington Works in 1848. Sold to Joseph Rodgers & Sons in 1971 and to Imperial Knife Co. in 1977. The I*XL trademark dates from 1787 and is still in use. Knives, Photo 195.

WYOMING RANCHMAN OUTFITTERS; Cheyenne, Wyoming
Acquired the equipment of F.A. Meanea about 1930 and remains in Western-wear business in Cheyenne. Watch Fobs, Photo 317.

WYOMING STATE PRISON; Rawlins, Wyoming
Bridles, Photos 72, 73, 76. Gun Rigs, Photo 178.

WYATT, CHARLES; Maybell, Colorado
Maker of bits and spurs from 1906 until the 1930s. Spurs, Photo 287.

X
Spur mark of Kelly Bros. Mfg. Co.

YORK, H.; Sheffield, England   Knives, Photo 196.

REFERENCES

Ahlborn, Richard E., editor. *Man Made Mobile*, Smithsonian, Washington, D.C., 1980.

Beatie, Russel H. *Saddles*, University of Oklahoma Press, Norman, 1981.

Beitz, Les. *Treasury of Frontier Relics*, Edwin House, New York, 1966.

Browning, John, and Gentry, Curt. *John M. Browning, American Gunmaker*, Doubleday, New York, 1964.

Burroughs, John Rolfe. *Where the Old West Stayed Young*, William Morrow, New York, 1962.

Cunningham, Eugene. *Triggernometry*. Caxton, Caldwell, Idaho, 1941.

Dorsey, R. Stephen. *American Military Belts and Related Equipments*, Pioneer Press, Union City, Tennessee, 1984.

Flayderman, Norm. *Flayderman's Guide to Antique American Firearms*, DBI, Northbrook, Illinois, 1987.

Forbis, William H., and editors. *The Cowboys*, Time Life Books, New York, (date 1973).

Foster-Harris. *The Look of the Old West*, Viking Press, New York, 1955.

Garvaglia, Louis A., and Worman, Charles G. *Firearms of the American West 1866-1894*, University of New Mexico Press, Albuquerque, 1985.

Goins, John. *Goins' Encyclopedia of Cutlery Markings*, Knife World Publications, Knoxville, Tennessee, 1986.

Grant, Bruce. *The Cowboy Encyclopedia*, Rand McNally, New York, 1951.

Harris, Allan. *The "Olde" Bridle Bit Collectors Guide*, author, Mark Twain Press, Arlington Heights, Illinois, 1985.

Haug, LeRoy C., and Malm, Gerhard. *Bible of Bridle Bits*, authors, Valley Falls, Kansas, 1975.

Heide, Robert, and Gilman, John. *Cowboy Collectibles*, Harper & Row, New York, 1982.

Hough, E. *The Story of the Cowboy*, D. Appleton & Co., New York, 1897.

Jacobs, Lee. *A McChesney Manual*, author, Colorado Springs, Colorado, 1988.

Ketchum, William C. Jr. *Western Memorabilia*, Hammond Inc., Maplewood, New Jersey, 1980.

Kopec, John et al. *Old West Antiques & Collectibles*, Great American, Austin, Texas, 1979.

Kopec, John et al. *A Study of the Colt Single Action Army Revolver*, authors, La Puente, California, 1976.

Laird, James R. *The Cheyenne Saddle*, author, Frontier Press, Cheyenne, Wyoming, 1982.

Levine, Bernard. *Levine's Guide to Knives and Their Values*, DBI, Northbrook, Illinois, 1985.

Madis, George. *The Winchester Book*, Art and Reference House, Brownsboro, Texas, 1977.

Maxwell, Gilbert S. *Navajo Rugs*, Best-West Publications, Palm Desert, California, 1963.

Mitchell, Natha McMinn. *Spur Marks*, author, Stanton, Texas, 1986.

Mora, Jo. *Trial Dust and Saddle Leather*, Charles Scribner's Sons, New York, 1946.

Nevin, David, and editors. *The Soldiers*, Time Life Books, New York, 1973.

Rice, Lee M., and Vernam, Glenn R. *They Saddled the West*, Cornell Maritime Press, Cambridge, Maryland, 1975.

Serven, James E. *Colt Firearms From 1836*, Stackpole Books, Harrisburg, Pennsylvania, 1979.

Steffen, Randy. *United States Military Saddles 1812-1843*, University of Oklahoma Press, Norman, Oklahoma, 1973.

Stephens, Frederick J. *Fighting Knives*, Arco Publishing, New York, 1985.

Sutherland, R.Q., and Wilson, R.L. *The Book of Colt Firearms*, authors, Kansas City, Missouri, 1971.

Trachtman, Paul, and editors. *The Gunfighters*, Time Life Books, New York, 1974.

VanMeter, David L. *G.S. Garcia, Elko, Nevada*, Anvil Publishing Co., Reno, Neveda, 1984.

Vernam, Glenn R. *Man on Horseback*, University of Nebraska Press, Lincoln, Nebraska, 1964.

Watts, Peter. *Dictionary of the Old West*, Promontory Press, New York, 1982.

Wilson, R.L. *The Colt Heritage*, Simon & Schuster, New York, 1979.